RENEWALS 458-4574

WITHDRAWN
UTSA LIBRARIES

THE INDIAN ENTREPRENEUR
A SOCIOLOGICAL PROFILE OF
BUSINESSMEN AND THEIR PRACTICES

Centre de Sciences Humaines (Centre for Social Sciences and Humanities): Created in New Delhi in 1989 the CSH, is part of network of research centres of the French Ministry of Foreign Affairs. The Centre's research work is primarily oriented towards the study of issues concerning the contemporary dynamics of development in India and South Asia. The activities of the Centre are focused on four main themes, namely: Economic growth and sustainable development, International and regional relations, Institutional structures and political constructions of identity and Urban dynamics.

(Centre de Sciences Humaines, 2, Aurangzeb Road, New Delhi 110011, India, Tel: (91 11) 23 01 62 59/23 01 41 73, Fax: (91 11) 23 01 84 80, E-mail: public@csh-delhi.com, Website: http://www.csh-delhi.com)

Institut Français de Pondichéry (French Institute of Pondicherry): Created in 1955, the IFP is a multidisciplinary research and advanced educational institute. Major research works are focusing on Sanskrit and Tamil languages and literatures—in close collaboration with the *Ecole Française d'Extrême-Orient*—ecosystems, biodiversity and sustainability, dynamics of population and socio-economic development.

(Institut Français de Pondichéry, 11, Saint Louis Street, P.B. 33 Pondicherry 605 001, Tel: (91 413) 23 34 170/23 34 168, Telex: 469224 FRAN-In, Fax: (91 413) 23 39 534, E-mail: ifpdir@ifpindia.org, Website: http://www.ifpindia.org.)

THE INDIAN ENTREPRENEUR

A Sociological Profile
of Businessmen and Their Practices

edited by

BRUNO DORIN

MANOHAR

CENTRE DE SCIENCES HUMAINES
2003

First published 2003

© Bruno Dorin, 2003

All rights reserved. No part of this publication may be
reproduced or transmitted, in any form or by any means,
without prior permission of the editor and the publisher

ISBN 81-7304-477-5

Published by
Ajay Kumar Jain for
Manohar Publishers & Distributors
4753/23 Ansari Road, Daryaganj
New Delhi 110 002

Typeset at
Digigrafics
New Delhi 110 049

Printed at
Lordson Publishers Pvt. Ltd.
Delhi 110 007

Library
University of Texas
at San Antonio

Contents

Foreword

This work developed from an idea that we at the Economics, Trade and Finance Commission of the Embassy of France in India had, namely to help our companies deal with the realities of the Indian market by providing them with the means for a better understanding of this complex society, and above all, of Indian enterprises, as future partners or future competitors.

For such a study to be really meaningful, it was necessary first to identify one or more researchers capable of visualizing the scope and nature of the work and, secondly, to ensure that there was sufficient backup support from the French firms present in India.

The response of the Centre de Sciences Humaines at New Delhi, and particularly of its incumbent director, Mr. Bruno Dorin, was quick and positive. Researchers were identified and approached, and despite the fact that they were busy with other projects, their interest in taking up the project was immediate. The team, with Bruno Dorin (Ph.D. economics) as coordinator, comprised Anne Vaugier-Chatterjee (Ph.D. political science), Pierre Lachaier (Ph.D. anthropology) and Nicolas Flamant (Ph.D. anthropology). The CSH's new director, Mr. Frédéric Grare, who took over from B. Dorin in April 1999, confirmed the Centre's support for the project.

No sooner had I conceived the project than the French firms based in India were contacted. Their reaction was instant and heartening, starting with the chairman of the Indian chapter of the French Foreign trade advisors, Mr. Jean-Michel Callot, then director-general of Alcatel India, and his successor, Mr. Marc Philippe, the representative of Suez-Lyonnaise des Eaux in India. The members of this section were easy to convince. As a result the necessary funds, including for my own participation, were immediately released. The total amount was promptly handed over to the CSH in order to minimize delay in initiating the study.

We now have a study that is ready—produced within a very short period—with an eminently practical objective, and by recognized social scientists, who showed great sensitivity to the concrete concerns of French entrepreneurs in their exploration of the Indian market. It is at the same time a work of erudition, intelligence, and utility for any action in the sphere of business. This is an example of a tripartite initiative comprising firms, French research groups in India and a department of the Embassy.

The plan of the work provides the reader with the necessary elements for an enlightened approach towards the Indian partner and a proper perception of the sociological components of his environment. It also helps in coming to grips with the human dimension of the market in a country in which France is planning to invest substantially in every way.

Jean-Charles Rouher
Head
Economics, Trade & Finance Commission
for France in India

Preface

This study was commissioned and financed by the fourteen French firms listed below, as well as by the Mission Economique et Financière of the French Embassy in India, headed by Mr. Jean-Charles Rouher, who has been the principal initiator and promoter of this work:

Aérospatiale–EADS, Alcatel Trade International, Alstom Limited, Crédit Lyonnais, Faurecia, Indo-French Chamber of Commerce and Industry, Lafarge Inde, Pernod Ricard India Liaison Service, Sanofi India Liaison Office, Société Générale Inde, SOFEMA, Suez–Lyonnaise des Eaux, Thomson CSF Liaison Office, Schneider Electric India.

The terms of the study were both ambitious and pragmatic: in the words of Jean-Charles Rouher, they were to 'bring out a document that, on the basis of data available on various Indian businessmen (geographical and social origins, religion, caste, education, family values, degree of internationalization, etc.), would enable one to paint a realistic picture of the attitude of these Indian businessmen towards (1) government officials (Union and federated states), (2) modern techniques of management, (3) economic liberalization and globalization, (4) research, (5) politics' (Note in French to the Centre de Sciences Humaines, 25 May 1998).

The study was conducted between September 1999 and May 2000, by a team formed and headed by Bruno Dorin: the first part of the research was entrusted to Pierre Lachaier, the second to Anne Vaugier-Chatterjee and the third to Nicolas Flamant, on the basis of their experience and expertise in the concerned fields. Several meetings punctuated the study and writing phases: these four scholars bear full responsibility for the opinions expressed in this document, not the organizations to which they are attached.

Contributors

BRUNO DORIN, born in 1966, has studied economics (Ph.D.), management and agricultural engineering. His doctoral thesis, sponsored by the Indian and French Governments, led him to spend two years in India (1990–1) to survey the oils and oilseeds industry of the country. In January 1995, he was appointed Director of the Centre de Sciences Humaines at New Delhi (CSH) by the French Ministry of External Affairs, in order to shift the research activities of this institute from ancient India (archaeology and Indo-Persian studies) towards contemporary India (economics, political science, international relations, sociology, etc.). He came back to France in September 2000 to teach Economics at the Ecole Supérieure d'Agriculture de Purpan (ESAP, Toulouse). He is now economist at CIRAD (Montpellier), and has published more than thirty articles in various journals, as well as a few books, mainly in food and agricultural economics.

NICOLAS FLAMANT, born in 1968, has a Ph.D. in social anthropology. He is a member of the Centre d'Anthropologie des Mondes Contemporaines at the Ecole des Hautes Etudes en Sciences Sociales (EHESS, Paris), and a director of projects at the Institut de Développement 'Entreprise et Personnel'. His research has focused on forms of power and social hierarchies in enterprise, in particular at managerial level. Along with the studies that he has undertaken in France, especially on firms promoting state-of-the-art technologies, Nicolas Flamant is interested in Indian enterprises that are entering international markets. Laureate of the 'Bourse Romain Rolland' (Ministry of External Affairs), this led him—in the context of a collaboration with the Institut Français de Pondicherry (IFP)—to carry out a field study lasting several months at Tholpuram in Tamil Nadu, on the leather industry and on shoe exports to the West.

PIERRE LACHAIER was born in 1946 at Calais. After studying engineering at the Ecoles des Hautes Etudes Industrielles, Lille, he worked for ten years in France and Switzerland in the R&D departments of several international chemical firms. He then spent two years in Maharashtra working for a non-government organization. Back in France, he prepared a *Diplôme d'Etudes Approfondies* in Ethnology (M.Phil.), and obtained his doctorate in Social Anthropology at the Ecole des Hautes Etudes en Sciences Sociales (*'Réseaux marchands et industriels au Maharashtra, Castes, sous-traitance et clientélisme'*). He is a member of the Centre d'Etude de l'Inde et de l'Asie du Sud (CEIAS, Paris) and disseminates his work through seminars and articles. In 1995, he joined the Ecole Française d'Extrême Orient (EFEO) and was assigned to the Centre d'Indologie of Pondicherry as researcher in social sciences. His book *Firmes et entreprises en Inde, La firme lignagère dans ses réseaux* (IFP-Karthala-EFEO, 1999) covers his principal works.

ANNE VAUGIER-CHATTERJEE has a degree from the Institut d'Etudes Politiques (IEP, Paris) and a Ph.D. in political science from the Ecole des Hautes Etudes en Sciences Sociales (EHESS, Paris). An India specialist, she is at present research coordinator at the Centre de Sciences Humaines in New Delhi. Her research focuses on contemporary Indian politics (parties and institutions). She has worked for several years on federalism in India, in particular on the Punjab crisis. She has published a book, *Histoire politique du Pendjab* (Paris: L'Harmattan, 2001) and several articles in academic journals such as *Hérodote, Cultures et Conflits, Pouvoirs* or *Historiens et Géographes*.

MAP OF INDIA: APPROXIMATE STATE-WISE DISTRIBUTION
OF KINSHIP SYSTEMS AND OF DRAVIDIAN AND
SANSKRITIC LANGUAGES

Source: Adapted from T.R. Trautmann, 'The Study of Dravidian Kinship',
in Patricia Uberoi (ed.): *Family, Kinship and Marriage in India*,
Oxford University Press, Delhi, 1993, p. 85.

Note: The external boundaries of India depicted in this map are neither
correct nor authentic.

We are grateful to the geomatics laboratory of the Institut
Français de Pondichery and to Mme M.-C. Guero for preparing a
map that unfortunately we have not been able to include here for
technical reasons.

Introduction

The business environment and markets of India are like a maze for most Western entrepreneurs. It is well known that India is a dense and complex mosaic of cultures, communities and religions, that drives some to despair by its archaisms, and overwhelms others with its astonishing modernity. We also know that Hinduism and the caste system have produced highly structured societies, of which we see only the caricature projected by a media in search of the exotic. But exotica is of no use when it comes to importing or exporting, investing capital or setting up a factory, developing a new product or service. And last but not least, we know that in India, once the initial enthusiasm of the first meetings wears off, building a partnership can turn out to be much more complicated than expected. It can even end in failure, a failure all the more sad and bitter given that we blame the 'irrationality' of the local modes of thinking and working. But these modes have in fact their own rationalities. At least that is what this small book will attempt to demonstrate by profiling Indian businessmen in their sociological environment. We are not asked to adopt their logic and practices, which is impossible, but at least to recognize that the latter follow a certain logic and that it is important and useful to grasp the principal dimensions of this logic.

Drawing sociological profiles of Indian businessmen remains an ambitious and tricky task. The cultural, sociological and economic diversity we find in India is also present in its industrialists, merchants and other contemporary businessmen. Some come from families still attached to tradition, whereas others are very Westernized and have been so for many generations. They could be heir to a secular family concern, or self-made men whose business took only a few years to flourish. The more prominent among them are likely to have studied in prestigious American, European or Indian business schools, or they could have given up their studies rather early. There is such a variety of examples that it is not possible to list them all.

However, in view of this great diversity it is interesting to highlight a common characteristic: these entrepreneurs were able to develop a business activity in India. This meant that they were able to cope with attitudes and perceptions peculiar to India, its history and its civilization. It is then very convenient for the analyst to dwell upon these specificities and 'traditions', and to disregard the 'modernism' and 'avant-garde' characteristics of many of the businessmen, as will be the case in this book too. But what is therefore important is to keep this narrowing of vision firmly in mind, all the more so because it is no longer possible to counter 'tradition' with 'modernity' in contemporary India, except perhaps for the convenience of language. Some types of half-forgotten knowledge are in fact re-integrated under a 'rationalized' form which, moreover, does not fail to inspire certain Western schools of management, while at the same time computers replace account books in rituals invoking the goddess of wealth.

This said, our enterprise is none the easier for it, for there are many ways of tackling the matter at hand. On the academic front, should one for example use the approach, concepts, and tools of the sociology of organizations, of industrial economics, of the anthropology of institutions, or of political science? By definition, all these disciplines study 'social facts', and each of them sheds a specific light on a particular subject. Which one should we choose? It is a difficult decision to make, especially as nothing should be *a priori* excluded, from private spheres to public policies, from cottage industries to big international groups, from agro-based industries to information technology, from the south to the north of the subcontinent, from Parsis to Kamma Naidus. . . . So, rather than cling to the rigour and formalism of academics, which would mean defining a problematic, a method, a specific field of investigation, we shall concentrate on another type of objective: scan a wide field of realities (i.e. open many doors that others can later push a little wider with their own means), while providing a practical guide of names and key concepts (which one can later return to according to circumstances and cases). In this perspective, this book will concentrate on three focal planes, each photographing certain realities which, together, should give at the end a rather good and global picture of the situation.

The first focal plane has a wide angle, because it exposes and explains some important components structuring the socio-cultural world of Indian businessmen, namely the family, the community and some of their 'value-concepts' (see Chapter I). Indeed, the Joint-Family is first and foremost a classical Indian institution that many traders and industrialists still tend to favour. The rules and prerogatives of this family structure must be clear, because the Hindu personal code depends on them, as well as the Joint Family Business and its specific manner of functioning. Moreover, most prominent business families can trace their origin back to certain castes—or communities—with a business calling, e.g. the Chettiars (Chidambaram group), Gujaratis (Ambani group), Marwaris (Birla group), Parsis (Tata and Godrej groups), Sindhis (Hinduja group). . . . These communities have frequently acquired a pan-Indian stature that is reflected in their diasporas spanning several continents. How are these networks established and organized? Finally, after having measured the family's importance and the roots it has within a community which often acts as a factor of identification, it is useful to specify some typical value-concepts. As a matter of fact, traders and entrepreneurs compete with each other for prestige, in particular during special occasions and 'semi-public' ceremonies, such as marriage, or donations to religious and charitable organizations. What are the grass roots of such behaviour? What does 'seva' (notion of service) mean today, besides inspiring new doctrines of work motivation in the corporate world, or even a way of salvation for the Indian nation on the battlefield of the world economy?

The second focal plane looks at the history of five prominent industrial families, in order to highlight some elements of the logic and constraints of organization and action in the Indian politico-economic space, from the struggle against colonization until the present time (see Chapter II). India is the birthplace of huge family-owned industrial empires, the most famous ones being those of Tata, Birla, Godrej, Bajaj and Ambani. These Indian titans of industry are today practically on an equal footing in terms of power and networks, but they do not for all that constitute a sociologically homogenous group. Who are they? How did they emerge on the national scene? What sort of relationship did they have with the various governments over the years? How were they involved in the economic policies of the country? Or, on the contrary, how did they fight governmental policies? From Congress hegemony to unstable government coalitions, from a planned economy to liberalization, several events have drastically altered their environment and influenced the running of their businesses. To trace this history is as fascinating as it is to understand, through it, the extent of the new challenges that these big business groups have now to face: economic liberalization, foreign competition and consolidation of the individual's culture within their own families.

Far from the administrative spheres of New Delhi and the commercial capital of Mumbai (Bombay), the final picture is a close-up of a leather industry (see Chapter III), where much of the work is subcontracted by foreign leather firms. It is located near Chennai (Madras) in Tamil Nadu. An in-depth study of this particular milieu and the special relationship developed with the owners and managers of this industry, have facilitated an insider-view of the behaviour patterns of Indian entrepreneurs in their work environment. It thus helps to reply to the many questions that occur at this level of observation. How and up to what point does the socio-religious background of these entrepreneurs (Muslims in this case) determine the organization and the management of the industrial tool (recruitment, capital associations, demand and supply networks, etc.)? Inversely, how does industrialization and market economy impose new working relationships (gender co-habitation, interaction between different castes and religious communities)? More generally, how does the Indian businessman integrate or adapt the imperatives of modern management, especially in this highly export-oriented sector where the international market imposes certain constraints which *a priori* are not very compatible with the traditional mores and hierarchies prevailing in India? Several answers to these key questions will be found in this third and final section, which also highlights the sociological and religious linkages of the dominant groups, the nature of their relationship with each other as well as with others, the levers of social advancement, the conflicts and contradictions derived from the international economic environment in which they henceforth evolve.

I. The Socio-Cultural World
Family, Community, 'Value-concepts'

PIERRE LACHAIER

The joint family and caste are two fundamental Indian institutions. These institutions have given rise to much controversy and will no doubt continue to remain emotionally-charged topics of discussion. They have been studied in classical works by philologists and jurists, and by anthropologists in field studies. The law deals with normative schemas that do not always reflect actual behaviour and customs, whereas anthropology tends to describe the latter in their infinite variety, according to regions and to social groups. Theories of evolution and modernization that moreover had supporters both in India and the West, predicted their gradual disappearance. But even though these institutions were undeniably transformed, they continue to play a not unimportant role in many aspects of social, political and economic life, as this first chapter illustrates in its presentation of the joint family (see pp. 19–32), castes and communities (see pp. 32–49) and some 'value-concepts' prevalent in the world of the captains of Indian industry (see pp. 50–62). Obviously we cannot claim to cover all the dimensions of this complex universe but, on the basis of empirical observation, we can examine some of them and note their more characteristic features. In this endeavour, we have based our study on examples drawn mostly from among the 50–100 biggest family businesses in the private sector.

THE INDIAN FAMILY

DESCENT AND MARRIAGE

Real or mythical lineages are mainly formed around the two *Lineages* axes of descent and marriage alliances. The continuity of generations is usually recognized through the male line, from father to son (patrilineal system), but in south India in particular, it can be through women (matrilineal system). Men who are related through successive filiations form a lineage. A lineage that can trace its genealogy a very long way back generally provides itself with an original ancestor, a mythical character who is often deified. It is then termed a clan. Thus, Brahmins claim that their clans go back to the ancient sages or *rishis*, who conceived or received the ancient Vedic texts. Some merchant groups, like the Lohanas of Gujarat claim to belong to the Sun clan, whose first ancestor was the god Rama (hero of the great epic *Ramayana*). The Nagarattar Chettiars are subdivided into nine clans corresponding to as many sub-divisions of Shivaite temples (Nishimura, 1998: 43). Smaller male lineages of two to four generations (or descent groups) underlie the institution of the family.

Elder and Younger

The maximum authority resides in the oldest male member of the line (the maternal uncle in a matrilineal system: there is no matriarchate). He must worship his direct ancestors through at least three generations, hence the importance of having a male line. The eldest brother with authority over the younger ones in the family often also wields it in the family business. Thus the younger brother, about forty years of age, who is the company manager, puts out his cigarette when his older brother unexpectedly enters his office, for one does not smoke in the presence of one's elders (though a guest is most welcome to smoke). In another business example, the older brother reserves the right of contacts with clients and suppliers, while the younger brother deals with the internal management of the enterprise. Over time, lineages are segmented into lines constituting a hierarchy, depending on whether they descend from an older or a younger brother. This hierarchical relationship—elder/younger—can also structure relations between enterprises, when for example it coincides with the relationship between a principal (elder brother) and a subcontractor (younger brother) in the small-enterprises sector. Family hierarchy imposes different obligations on brothers. The eldest, destined to succeed the father at the helm of the family business, has less time than his juniors to start new enterprises. But once these are successfully established, it is the older son who takes over from the younger brother who founded the business (Lachaier, 1999: 244).

The relationship between brothers and sisters is celebrated some days after the new year festival of Diwali (Dipawali). The brother goes to the sister's house with gifts, eats with her, while the sister ties a coloured cotton thread around his wrist. The brother–sister tie is sometimes solid enough to found an industrial group on the strength of the relationship—or to be exact, with the help of the sister's husband. For instance, a small industrialist from Pune was of the opinion that the brother–sister linkage is stronger than the relationship between husband and wife, for, he argued, it is the brother who presents the 'fiancée' for marriage to her future husband and, according to custom, when the sister comes back to the maternal home for her delivery, he sees the child being born and develops a strong emotional bond with it. In fact, the sisters in question probably hold a share of the capital of the industrial group, and their children, whose maternal uncle he is, are potentially those whom his own children would find suitable for marriage (see Chapter III) (Lachaier, 1999: 223–7).

Brothers and Sisters

In Brahmanical doctrine, marriage, which was usually conceived as a sort of 'gift' of the young virgin, was particularly meritorious from a spiritual point of view. It has preserved its sacramental character and remains one of the most important rites in the life of the individual and the family. The very opulence of the festivities on this occasion often serves to enhance the family's social prestige. This can be important for the credit they enjoy in some sectors of activity where many transactions are based on trust. In December 1989, the Shahs, who are among the biggest Gujarati Jain diamond merchants of Palanpur, invited some 15,000 people to their daughter's wedding, held in a Bombay stadium. So much money was spent that it caused an outcry, and the police had to intervene to clear the stadium entrance of demonstrators (Piramal, 1996: 315–17). Marriages are for the most part arranged, even among the more Westernized Indian families. They are like a strategic alliance between two families, or even between two descent groups. A romantic involvement is not excluded, but it is believed that a relationship which grows out of the closeness resulting from the union of bride and bridegroom, will be more lasting than one where the involvement exists prior to it. In fact, the two families make sure that the horoscopes of the

Marriage

fiancés are compatible, and today, matrimonial registers compiled by caste associations even indicate the blood group of members.

Exogamy-
Endogamy

The marriages nearly always take place outside one's clan (the exogamy principle), but into a wider kinship group (caste, see pp. 32–49), or into a subdivision of the caste (the endogamy principle). In 1996, the three sons of the London-based Sindhi Hinduja family were married on the same day. Two of these unions, it is said, were love marriages, but all three wives are Sindhis, one from Casablanca, and the other two from Bombay. Family opposition to an inter-caste marriage of their progeny can be strong enough to lead to suicide (Dutta, 1997: 247–8). Marwari Maheshwari caste organizations organize matrimonial fairs, the most famous of which takes place at Indore in Madhya Pradesh. Patronized by the caste's economic élite for the benefit of its less well-off members, the Indore fair, in 1994, attracted more than 1,500 Maheshwari hopefuls, mostly from the neighbouring states. The organizers publish illustrated catalogues, with a special section for disabled persons (Pache, 1998).

Marriage
Preferences

There exist many kinship systems in India of which the two most important are those prevailing in the northern and the southern belts (Karve, in Uberoi, 1993: 50–73). Their geographical spread corresponds roughly to the Sanskritic and Dravidian linguistic areas (see Map on p. 13) (Trautman, in Uberoi, 1993: 84). But intermediary cases can also be found (for instance, Maharashtra where the language is Sanskritic and the kinship system of the Dravidian type); also regional kinship patterns differ at the local level according to caste, class and sectarian affiliations. In the north–south kinship systems, the principal difference is based on the type of marriage alliance. In north India, the husband is generally from a subdivision of higher social status than his wife's (the hypergamic alliance), who herself is from a subdivision of the husband's caste (for example among Patel or Patidar Gujarati merchants) (Pocock, in Uberoi, 1993: 330–40), or eventually from another caste (women of the Arora caste often tend to marry men from the Khatri caste) (Singh, 1998: 127). The matter is more complex in south India where the tendency is to marry relatives from already allied descent groups of equal status (the isogamic alliance). For example, it is proper for a man to marry a cross-cousin, or a niece whose maternal uncle he is. A man's cross-cousins are the daughters of his mother's brothers (his maternal uncles), or the daughters of his father's sisters (his paternal aunts). All marriage unions do not correspond to this type of marriage preference, and with Westernization, there is a tendency to marry outside the kinship group. There have been many instances of marriages between cross-cousins in the genealogy of the great banker and merchant, Raja Sir Annamalai Chettiar. His descendants include three parliamentarians, consul generals, businessmen controlling several of the big industrial groups of Tamil Nadu, some of them connected through cross-cousin marriages (Nishimura, 1998: 89). Today polygyny[1] (one man and several wives) is illegal, the exception being Muslims and some tribal societies. It was often practised when the first wife was sterile, and sometimes with her consent. The second wife had an inferior position in the husband's descent group and could come from a group of inferior status. When their second wife comes from the temple dancers' community (*devadasi*) of the Isai Vellalar caste, the Chettiar Nagarattar may have close access to the movie industry (Nishimura, 1998: 60). As the Nagarattars do not consider the children of these inter-caste unions suitable marriage partners, they tend to form a subdivision of inferior status.

The vocabularies of kinship are much richer in the Indian than in the European languages. They include specific terms of address and reference for maternal and paternal cousins, for brothers and sisters, according to whether they are older or not, etc. An analysis of these terms shows that they reflect corresponding kinship structures: in north India, kinship terminology differentiates between parents and in-laws, whereas in south India, it distinguishes the relatives who are marriageable from those who are not. In other words, social relationships are well reflected in linguistic usages. In the Dravidian type of marriage there is a tendency for the family circle to become more close-knit from one generation to the next, as its members can be

Kinship and Capital

---

[1] Two forms of polygamy are practised in India, polygyny (one man and several wives), and polyandry (one woman and several husbands). Polyandry is chiefly practised in the Himalaya and in some tribal societies.

related to each other in more ways than one. On the contrary, marriage in the north incorporates new relatives into the family group and widens the circle of exchange. If certain business groups in the south, mostly Chettiars, have been less subject to the sort of divisions that have affected groups in the north since Independence, it is, so it is believed, because the underlying kinship structure in the south is more solid (Tripathi, 1999: 31). Whether it be north or south, kinship relationships between descent groups can be matched by corresponding cross-investments: the wife's capital and dowry can become part of the head of the family's firm's capital. As the various kinship categories generally have differing degrees of trust associated with them, lenders and bankers have drawn inspiration from them to build and differentiate their capital aggregates (Rudner, 1995: 101–2).

THE HINDU JOINT FAMILY IN CLASSICAL WRITINGS

Hindu Law

The family in India is governed by the Hindu, Muslim and Christian personal (not territorial) laws, which have their roots in corresponding religious and customary texts. Hindu family law applies also to Jains, Sikhs and Buddhists. It originates from two schools of interpretation of ancient texts, the Dayabhaga, followed mainly in Bengal, and the Mitakshara, which is practised in most of the rest of India. Here we will study the Hindu family and laws as prescribed by the Mitakshara (Jhabvala, 1996). It should be noted that in Indian law it is the undivided Hindu family (Hindu Joint Family or HJF)[2] that is considered first and not the individual, as in Western laws. Moreover, it correlatively defines the rights of its members over its undivided assets, or coparcenary.

Karta

The HJF includes all those people who are descended from a common ancestor, with their wives and unmarried daughters, who eventually become members of the HJF of their husbands once they are married. The oldest male member becomes the *karta* or head of the HJF. He manages the family business and the pooled income of the members, that he then redistributes

---

[2] Also called 'Hindu Undivided Family', 'HUF'.

among them in accordance with their needs, and not according to their share in the inheritance. In industrial and merchant families, the *karta* is usually the manager of the companies and firms controlled by family members. His powers are vast and irrevocable. He can alienate the assets of the HJF in its interests with the consent of the coparceners. The HJF is not limited in number or in time; inheritance, kitchen and cult are common. The HJF is not a legal entity distinct from the members that compose it.

The coparcenary is formed of members of the HJF, with undivided rights of property and possession on its patrimony. It includes only sons, grandsons and great-grandsons of the common ancestor, that is, three successive generations of men in the patrilineal line. The women of the HJF have the privilege of being looked after, but they are not members of the coparcenary. The shares of the members of the coparcenary in the undivided inheritance vary in time according to the births and deaths that occur. In principle inalienable, they can nevertheless be transferred or gifted with the consent of all the coparceners. The coparcenary is a distinct legal entity that can enter into a contract or take legal action. The rights of the coparcenary are distinct from the individual property rights, or self-acquired assets of the members of the HJF. These separate rights are freely alienable by their holders; they cannot be shared by the members of the HJF without the holders' consent. However, the jewellery acquired by the women are generally the most important objects over which they have a separate right. In the HJF of the Bajaj family, the share of the wealth given to the women for purchasing jewellery is fixed by the family council, and in the Mittal family, it is divided equally among the daughters-in-law (Gurcharan Das, 1996: 75, 79).

Co-parcenary

The Hindu is born with several pious obligations and responsibilities that are considered his debts (*rin*).[3] Inspired by religious concepts, the law obliges the descendants of the *karta* to reimburse the real debts that he may have contracted legally

Debts

---

[3] The concept of 'duty' or 'obligation' is very deep-rooted; it takes precedence over that of 'right', as in all traditional laws.

on behalf of the HJF. Small financial family concerns such as the Hindu Joint Family Business (HJFB) stress the solidarity of their members for the benefit of their creditors, in contrast to the limited responsibility of private limited firms (Lachaier, 1999: 131–6). Private limited firms, today governed by the Companies Act of 1956, did not have an equivalent in India, where most businesses were partnerships or HJFBs. It should be noted that members of the HJF, or the HJF itself, can enter into a partnership with each other or with a third person. The rules and regulations governing the HJFB fall under family law, with the addition of some special provisions (Diwan, 1995: 161–73). Inheritance and succession laws are complex; in general, the sons receive equal shares, and the eldest son becomes the *karta*.

Property
(Joint and Individual)

Studies have shown that the proportion of joint families is relatively small. But members of families who are physically and legally separated, can still show great solidarity and maintain very close relations with each other. Two or more households belonging to the same HJF can reside under different roofs situated in the same area, locality, and even in the same building in the case of apartments. Male members who have separated from the HJF can have individual property rights, distinct from the rights of the coparceners. Separate households, individual property-owners and coparceners thus constitute different groups born from the same HJF. Also, single families originating from the HJF can each reconstitute an undivided family in two or three generations.

THE HINDU JOINT FAMILY IN DAILY LIFE

Family
and
Business

Businesses were nearly always created by a joint family who found it advantageous to remain so in the interests of the business.[4] To forge large groups, industrialists firstly applied for funds from their close relatives and secondly from families allied

---

[4] Cf. the studies conducted—the first one at Okhla, Delhi (Shrinivas, 1966: 83), and the other in Madras (now Chennai) (Singer, 1972: 286)—at a time when the undivided family was expected to disappear in industry. Shrinivas and Singer are quoted by Madan (1993: 432).

by marriage, before going to financial institutions (Dutta, 1997: 93). Until the 1960s at least, the chances were that the majority shareholders in many banks were also members of the same community, sometimes that of the entrepreneur himself (Thingalaya, 1999). Thus, Godrej is still one of the most important clients of the Zoraastrian Co-operative Bank Ltd., an institution started by Parsis primarily to serve the community (Bana, 1999: 101). In the following pages, we will take up the cases of the Bajaj family of Pune and the Mittals of Bombay,[5] each of whom control companies that rank among the fifty biggest Indian industrial groups. The Bajajs are the third-largest producers of motorized vehicles in the world: scooters, motor-cycles and auto-rickshaws (cf Chapter II). The Mittal's Ispat group is more diversified and is into construction, paper-making, shipping containers, socks, woven bags, etc.

The undivided family is above all a cultural milieu for all the members who have grown up in it, and sometimes have not had many opportunities to leave it. The values instilled by the founder contribute to family solidarity, stresses R. Bajaj, the *karta*, talking of his grandfather's ethos. One of his cousins adds to the theme by invoking the exemplary austerity of Mahatma Gandhi, whom his founder grandfather helped in his fight against the British. The Bajajs generally go on holiday together. At the Mittals, the children have grown up in the same house, have attended the same schools, and have the same outlook on life: 'We have a common outlook. We are homogenous', said one Mittal. The Mittal family of Bombay continues to live together and run a common kitchen.[6] There are three generations and sixty-nine family members: the mother, five uncles and five aunts from the first generation, sixteen brothers and cousins and wives of fifteen of them from the second generation, and thirty-one children of the third generation (some children do not live in Bombay and their married sisters have

Community Life

---

[5] As described in the interviews that Gurcharan Das (1996: 72–81), published in a revue brought out by the Marwari community, to which the Bajajs and Mittals belong.

[6] We do not know if there is a common cult; other big business families of Bombay have an in-house temple.

left the family). The Mittals live together in the twenty-one apartments in their three towers. Until 1984, they took their meals together, prepared in the common kitchen. But because the family kept expanding, each household now has food brought from the common kitchen to their respective apartments. The individual kitchens with which all their apartments are equipped have only a secondary use. The fifty odd domestic staff take their food from this common kitchen. Forty chauffeurs are also employed.

Common Fund

The male members of the Bajaj and Mittal families all have major responsibilities in one or more companies of the family business group. The income from these companies of different sizes is pooled and redistributed under the *karta's* authority to the households and family members. To take an example, the Bajajs had allotted a certain sum to a tennis-playing son, to enable him to prepare for a tournament, which he won. But he could not keep the prize, as the elders decided to put it into the common account in keeping with the rules of the HJF. Thus, income earned by one member, but from an activity financed by the pooled income of the HJF, is returned to it. And it is the same with the dividends of the Bajaj-Auto company, we are told.

Equal Treatment

During the Diwali festivities, under the *karta's* aegis, the Bajajs review all the rules governing the family, and decide the amount of money allocated for holidays, jewellery for the women, and for the personal expenditure of all its members. Whatever the size of the firm managed by each one, the nature of their function or their expertise, the sums allocated for personal expenditure are the same, both for the Bajajs and the Mittals. A Mittal explained: 'We give everyone a lot of space. Some of us really slog at work. Others enjoy themselves. Yet they earn the same, because they are family. We recognize that people are different. There is no sense trying to force unity.' The members interviewed among the Bajaj and Mittal families were emphatic about equal treatment. They felt that its observance was necessary if the family was to maintain its unity.

Status and Function

The normative model of the HJF simultaneously posits that: (1) the group takes precedence over the individual; (2) the group has a hierarchy according to sex and age; and (3) that every individual has inalienable rights over his self-acquired assets. The structure of the Bajaj and Mittal families corresponds to the normative model with one exception: those interviewed did not allude to the respect owed to their elders, which for them is taken for granted. The family remains a group with a status-based hierarchy, and whatever their age, junior members are subordinated to their elders. In the professional sphere, however, there reigns a function-based hierarchy in accordance with the individual's ability and position. The hierarchies of status and function are fundamentally incompatible, for one is founded on the primacy of the group while the other is based on that of the individual and the chances of their reconciliation are slim (an older member may have less ability than his younger relative on the professional plane but have a higher social status). For the HJF to be stable, an ideal separation between the familial and professional domains should be maintained, but without going so far as to disassociate one from the other. This is of course difficult as family members are inclined to project the hierarchy existing in the professional sphere into the family sphere: 'When things begin to go sour, . . . family life is . . . an anxiety-generating discipline with each one's performance constantly on the line. Brothers deal with brothers with a smile, but they make sure they bring a witness. At that point, "cruel is the quarrel of brothers", says Aristotle', and conversely in families more bound by tradition than the Bajajs. All things considered, the business HJF can be a harmonious entity only if, first, the family has greater value than the business, and secondly, if the status-hierarchy prevails in the family domain and the job-related hierarchy in the professional domain. This implies that the individual accepts being subordinated to the family, as must also the *karta*, who has always to give priority to the HJF and act for its good and in its best interests, *noblesse oblige*.

Evolution of the Hindu Joint Family

Both the Mittals and the Bajajs reiterated the necessity of strict equality in the allocation of sums for personal expenditure, if family harmony was to be maintained: it is because one is a member of the family that one has the right to the same

Sharing of Responsibilities

personal allocation, independent of economic performance. In other words, within the family, status is much more important than function, and the sphere of economic relations remains subordinate to that of primary social relations. But the day the sons demand an allocation, no longer the same for all, but proportionate to the income generated by each one towards the assets of the HJF—which would mean a major upheaval of the status hierarchy, the mainstay of the reigning order within the family group—the HJF would probably break up. Such a demand would imply the rise of a form of individualism in the claimant, which might be too powerful to remain contained in the domain that the family has reserved for him. To prevent quarrels between brothers from degenerating into such demands, the *kartas* try to allow members of the HJF to keep relatively autonomous fields of activity. At the Mittals, where the business is divided geographically and functionally, nephews are encouraged to develop their own businesses. But they must provide a regular account of their activities to the uncles, of whom the oldest is the *karta* by right (the father has expired). The uncles make collective decisions.

Diversifi-cation

Since Independence, and particularly over the 1980s–90s, the HJF has evolved, as is evident from a study of the rules of a HJF of Madras-based industrialists, dating from the 1950s–60s (Singer, 1968: 441). These rules stipulate that no member of the family should have personal assets, or individual investments separate from the joint investments, nor maintain a separate bank account. Moreover, financial transactions must be executed within everyone's knowledge. All profits must be reinvested in the family business, whose shares are handed down exclusively to descendants in the male line. The sons' wives have the right to a fixed allocation for household expenses, as well as for entertainment and travel. According to these rules, described as 'disciplinarian' by the descendants, the professional and family spheres were scarcely dissociated. The family hierarchy was much more rigid than that of the Mittal and Bajaj families, and the sons had practically no autonomy. In the HJFs studied, the new *karta* had to give the sons some degree of autonomy and entrust the third generation with special projects in order to prevent the group from breaking up after the death of the head of the family (Singer, 1968: 442). In the 1990s, the Mittals followed the same tactic. But this resulted in greater diversification of the group's activities, which today would be well advised to focus on its principal activity. The problems posed by the third generation of the HJF require more careful handling than in the past.

Since Independence, and especially during the 1980s–90s a growing number of undivided industrial families have wound up their HJF and divided their industrial empire among the members (*Business Today*, 1998: 44–5). Among the 100 most important Indian business groups, five belong to the Birla family, two are from the Goenkas, two from the Chhabrias, etc. (*Business Today*, 1997: 220–7). Only too often did these divisions occur on the basis of the interests of family members, rather than that of the companies and their shareholders. But sometimes, the dismembered branches continue to maintain good relations. Thus, the sons of the Agarwal family, once an HJF, have decided to federate as solidly as possible the nineteen companies of the group founded by Bhoruka, whose descendants they are (Dutta, 1997: 94). After the economic liberalization of 1991, the big family-owned concerns are having a difficult time because of increasing international competition and globalization of the economy. They are criticized for excessive diversification, for putting incompetent relatives in positions of authority, for producing technically outdated goods of average quality, for paying poor dividends to their shareholders, for diverting company profits, etc. The most pessimistic analysts predict their decline, if not their disappearance in the near future, at least in the joint family form.[7] But this is perhaps forgetting a little too soon that the joint family is predisposed to a tri-generational cycle of disintegration and reconstruction, and that several industrial groups of small to medium size, all or nearly all family concerns, will surface at the top of the list as the biggest groups in a few years. The controversy over the advantages and disadvantages of family businesses, of the '*Karta*

Family Disintegration

---

[7] Gurcharan Das, ex-CEO of Procter & Gamble, summarizes the situation in his article 'The Problem' (*Seminar*, No. 482, October 1999: 12–21). Other articles on this subject can be found in practically all the documents mentioned, namely *Business Today* (1997 and 1999) and Dutta (1997). See also Lachaier (1999: 339–44).

System of Management' as the late industrialist Santanu L. Kirloskar used to say, is not new (Lachaier, 1999: 182). It does not seem that its recent revival has greatly contributed to changing the usual lines of argument.[8]

CASTES AND COMMUNITIES

FAMILY, CASTE AND CLASS

Family and Caste

The Hindu Joint Family encompasses a large group of relatives, defined more in genealogical terms than through the inter-actions of its members with each other those of the HJF (Madan, in Uberoi, 1993: 419). It is at the level of this extended kinship group that one identifies oneself as a member of a clan, which is itself a subdivision of a larger group, the caste or the community. From the British colonial period until today, thousands of castes and communities have been listed by the Census of India (Singh, 1998); but those Indian entrepreneurs who, from the late nineteenth century onwards, founded large industrial groups, came from only a handful of them, with a reputation for their commercial calling (the so-called trading castes or business communities). We are going to talk of the better-known of such castes or communities, but first we may ask, what is a caste? Before replying to this question, it is important to spell out the difference between status and class.

Status and Class

Contemporary Indian society can be said to be composed of status groups and/or social classes. An individual's or a group's status is a socially-recognized hereditary attribute, whereas the fact of belonging to a social class depends in principle on acquired skills. Status and class qualify the individual's position in his social group differently. If social stratification into classes is defined mainly in terms of income and economic relations,

[8] This discussion was revived by the changing economic circumstances, and in particular by liberalization of the capital markets. The journal *Fortune India* published an article aggressively titled, 'Licence to Kill' (15 September 1996), whose authors are happy with the new rules which allow takeover bids on the least performing family groups, groups whose shareholders have lost quite a bit of money.

status hierarchy is generally influenced by criteria of a religious nature. Schematically speaking, a Brahmin industrialist belongs to a status group situated at the top of the social hierarchy because he is considered ritually pure. A low-caste industrialist, however, finds himself at the bottom end of the ladder, although he is from the same social class, as for example, when their enterprises and incomes are of equal size.[9] Sociological analyses in terms of status or class are complementary, although their effectiveness varies according to the scale of observation, the object observed, and the hypotheses that guide the study. The descriptions of industrialists and traders, generally characterized in terms of class, will in this study be defined in terms of status. Let us also note that the notion of 'acquired social position', correlative to that of social class, implies that the individual is given greater importance than the group to which he belongs; but in India, it is generally the inverse that applies, even if the group frequently gives the individual some room for independent action.

CASTES AND COMMUNITIES

The first Portuguese colonizers observed that Indian society   *Caste*
had numerous and distinct social groups, which they called 'castes'. Today the word 'caste' is used very generally and can refer to several levels of social differentiation. Sometimes it refers to broad pan-Indian social subdivisions of the *varnas*, while at other times it designates the *jati*, i.e. the social group which Indians identitify with from birth. But *jati* is itself a subdivision of a larger group with rather blurred contours, and which is also called caste. The successive order of inclusion of the subdivisional levels gives us the *varnas*, castes and *jatis*. The word 'community' is equated with caste, or it can have an even more general meaning (as in 'the business community').

In ancient literature, Indian society was shown to be composed   Varna
of four main social groups, or *varnas*, ranked according to their

[9] In 1985–6, Kolhapur leather industrialists from the lowest castes felt that they were being somewhat kept at a distance by their industrialist colleagues from the highest castes, who dominated the local chambers of commerce (study conducted P. Lachaier).

function in society. The first *varna* was that of the Brahmins; they had a sacerdotal role and were therefore required to study the Vedic texts. The second was that of the Kshatriya princes and warriors, whose duty was to maintain law and order in society. The third *varna*, that of the Vaishyas, was constituted by those who had an important economic function: landed farmers, merchants, and the professions. Members of the first three *varnas* were supposed to be twice-born (*dvija*) because they had undergone an initiation of which the string worn across the chest was the symbol. Taken together, they contrasted with the fourth *varna*, which consists of those who are at their service, the Shudras. The populations that were not included in these categories were considered as being outside the *varnas*: these were the Chandalas, the lowest castes who were called 'Untouchables'[10] in the British period. These old concepts were again brought into common usage in the nineteenth century, and in common parlance they are still referred to in this fashion, although one cannot really identify the social groups corresponding to the *varnas*. In addition, these references have regional variations. In Tamil Nadu and Pondicherry, where the Kshatriya and Vaishya *varnas* are supposed to be practically non-existent, people differentiate between the Brahmin and the Shudra *varnas* on the one hand, and the diverse lowest castes on the other. Let us reiterate that if the *varnas* still serve as a reference for the purpose of identity or prestige, they do not have any proven empirical reality today, except perhaps when they serve to differentiate from the lowest castes.

Jati

We do not really know if ancient Indian society was structured on the basis of the *varnas*, but what is certain is that at the beginning of the colonial period it was composed of castes or communities that had several levels of subdivisions. The most important observational level of subdivision was the *jati*. Traditional *jatis* shared four main characteristics, many of which are still observable:

---

[10] The words 'untouchables' or *parias* are no longer accepted in India. M.K. Gandhi called them Harijans, 'the children of God', but 'Dalits' seems now to be the term in general use (originally, name given by the Mahars of Maharashtra to their political movement), or, in administrative language, 'Scheduled Caste' (SC).

(1) they were exclusive from the point of view of marriage and commensality (meals were not shared, nor was water drunk with people from an inferior *jati*);

(2) the *jati* members exercised a professional activity or a specialization (there were *jatis* of oil-millers, sweetmeat makers, jewellers, traders, bankers, etc.); the activity served as a social indicator—*jati* members were supposed to practise it, even if in reality they did not do so;

(3) *jatis* were ranked, apart from other criteria, according to their degree of ritual purity: Brahmins were at the top of the social hierarchy, and the lowest caste, considered impure, at the bottom;

(4) *jatis* were often subdivided into clans, which were segmented into lineages and these into descent groups and extended families: ideally, the *jati* was conceived as an extended kinship group (in fact, genealogies were often fabricated for reasons of prestige); on the other hand, *jatis* were themselves regional subdivisions of bigger groups—castes and sub-castes.

Jatis can also be subdivided according to the religion of their members, into Hindu and Jain, or Hindu and Sikh sections, or more rarely into Hindu and Christian. Members of the same *jati*, even if they belong to different religious sections, can intermarry. Here *jati* is more important than religious affiliation. Christians and Muslims were also, and still are, subdivided into hierarchical sects and groups, although in a manner different from Hindus. Sometimes *jati* affiliations continue to separate Christians into lowest and upper castes, and it also happens that particular groups are considered lower by those of a higher status.[11]

Religion and Jati

The *jatis* often strove for admission into a higher social status by collectively practising a strategy known as Sanskritization. This consisted of adopting religious and dietary practices (vegetarianism) of the upper castes, and proceeding by successive reclassifications from one subdivision to another of

Sanskritization and Westernization

[11] The criteria and levels of subdivisions are too numerous for a global graphic representation, or even a schematic one, to be possible.

higher status. Thus, in the nineteenth century, the Nadars of Tamil Nadu, whose occupation was to collect palm juice, were considered the lowest of the low castes. But towards the beginning of the twentieth century, they slowly graduated to practising trade and industry, and today their politicians try and claim a Kshatriya origin for their caste. The strategies of social mobility have become more individualistic. Often they imply a certain Westernization of mores and a modern education. In the great metropolitan centres, prohibitions of contact have practically disappeared in public spaces, which means that meals can be taken together in restaurants, and one is not concerned with the *jati* of those with whom one has casual relations. The behaviour patterns typical of the *jati*, though generally harmless, but which can sometimes take a violent turn, are still the norm in villages and in provincial towns.

Caste Associations

Everywhere, even among those who have received a Western-type education, one continues to marry within the *jati*. Several *jati* associations have compiled, and now computerized pan-Indian—and even international—records of their members in order to facilitate the search for suitable life partners. The *jati* is also a network of mobilizable relations, especially useful in politics, and also in business (although here its workings are more discreet). For example, the Sindhis of Ulhasnagar (near Bombay) have published a business directory on their community for limited distribution. Apart from this, in a spirit of justice, the government has awarded certain socio-economic privileges to the Dalits and to other underprivileged social groups, by way of retrospective compensation. Members of social groups classified as 'Scheduled Castes and Tribes' (lowest castes and tribal populations), 'Backward Classes' (various low castes), 'Other Backward Classes' (medium-level castes), have the right to quotas and to reservations in universities, administrative jobs in the government, etc. The percentage of the population benefiting from compensatory privileges can be as high as 60 per cent or more in some states (Assayag, 1995). The demand for a recognized status corresponding to these categories has become a major political issue all over India.

MERCHANT CASTES

Whether they are old or recent, big or small, rich or medium-rich or poor, merchant castes and communities are divided and subdivided into groups (see Table 1) with a tendency towards endogamy. And often, only a few of these subdivisions specialized in trade, whereas others continued to earn their living from agriculture and cottage industries, or came to swell the ranks of the urban middle-class. Some castes, originally peasants, grew affluent towards the turn of the century (for instance, the Kamma Naidus of Coimbatore in Tamil Nadu; the Rajus and the Reddy(ar)s of Andhra Pradesh; the Patels of Gujarat). The conditions of others, conversely, have deteriorated, while yet others, in the aftermath of political upheavals, decreased in number because of the migration of their élites (the case of the Memon Muslims who migrated to Pakistan), and even, in some cases, disappeared from the Indian scene (Armenians and Baghdadi Jews). It is convenient to classify merchant castes according to their region of origin and their religious affiliation. But such a classification will always be an approximation because of repeated migrations (some castes called 'Punjabi', originally came from Rajasthan), and also a complex affair because of the different religious affiliations prevailing within the same caste: the Marwaris' and Banias' *jatis* comprised Hindu and Jain sections that can intermarry, and Punjabi castes have Hindu and Sikh sections. Few in number, the Jains have their own subdivisions, namely the Svetambara and Digambara. We will first take up the castes from north India, after which some castes from south India will be presented. The last section is reserved for Brahmin entrepreneurs and Muslim groups, found both in the north and the south.

Castes and Merchant World

MERCHANT CASTES AND COMMUNITIES
OF NORTH INDIA

There were supposed to be 128 merchant *jatis* or castes in Rajasthan (Todd, 1914), of which the Agarwal, the Maheshwari and the Oswal are best known. Globally designated as 'Marwari' from the time of the Mughal emperors Akbar and Shahjahan, the merchants of these castes were originally from Marwar (formally the state of Jodhpur) and from the Shekhwati region

Marwari

TABLE 1: PRINCIPAL MERCHANT CASTES AND COMMUNITIES OF INDIA

Castes and Communities	Subdivisions	H	Ja	S	Z	Mi	Ma	Je	C	Origin (O.) Present location (L.)
Marwari	Agarwal, Maheshwari, Oswal, etc.	+	+							O. Rajasthan L. India
Gujarati Bania	Various Meshri Various Shravak	+	+							O. Gujarat L. India
Parsi	Priests/Laymen				+					O. Iran, Gujarat L. Bombay, Gujarat, USA
Punjabi	Khatri Arora Agarwal	+ + +	+ 	+ + +						O. Punjab: Lahore, Multan, Delhi. L. Delhi, North India
Bhatia and Lohana	Kutchi, Halay, Sindhi	+								O. Sindh, Kutch, Saurashtra, L. Bombay, Gujarat, East Africa
Sindhi	Migrants from Pakistan	+								O. Sindh L. India, International Diaspora
Chettiar	Nagarattar	+								O. & L. Tamil Nadu

Castes and Communities	Subdivisions	H	Ja	S	Z	Mi	Ma	Je	C	Origin (O.) Present location (L.)
Kamma	Naidu	+								O. Andhra Pradesh. L. Andhra Pradesh, Tamil Nadu.
Nadar		+								O. & L. Tamil Nadu
Brahmins of Karnataka	Gaud Saraswat	+								O. & L. Karnataka, Maharashtra
Brahmins of Maharashtra	Deshastha, Konkanastha	+								O. & L. Maharashtra Bombay, Pune
Brahmins of Tamil Nadu	Iyer, Iyengar	+								O. & L. Tamil Nadu
Muslims	Memon Khoja, Bohora					+	+			O. Gujarat L. Bombay, Karachi, East and South Africa, Canada, UK
Christians	Armenian Syrian								+ +	L. Have left India O. Kerala L. South India
Jews	Baghdadi							+		L. Have left India

Note: (H) Hindu, (Ja) Jain, (S) Sikh, (Z) Zoroastrian, (Mi) Sunni Muslim, (Ma) Shia Muslim, (Je) Jew, (C) Christian.

(Jaipur and Bikaner states). For a long time they practised banking, trade, money-lending, and tax-farming for the princes and overlords of Rajasthan. Marwari migratory movements go a long way back in time. They came to Bengal in the middle of the sixteenth century as purveyors to the Rajput army raised by the Mughal emperor. During the colonial era, Calcutta became their most important trading centre. But from 1800, and more so from 1860 to 1900, the Marwaris also migrated in large numbers to Karachi, Bombay, Pune, Nagpur, Hyderabad, Mysore, Delhi, and from Calcutta to Assam and Rangoon (Burma). Dealing in domestic trade and export–import, banking, foreign exchange, moneylending, etc., they accumulated vast fortunes, particularly in Calcutta where they speculated in jute and soon were second only to the British. It is only after World War I that they began to set up industries. After Independence, the more important Marwari entrepreneurs, such as the Birlas, Singhanias, Dalmias, Bajajs, Goenkas, started to invest heavily in industry. Founder of an empire that today numbers some 200 companies, G.D. Birla started his career in pre-Independence Calcutta as a broker in the jute trade. He also funded much philanthropic work, and built many temples in different regions of India. Before the division of the family in 1986, the Birla group, flag bearer of the Hindu Marwari business community, was one of the biggest in India along with that of the Tatas.

Gujarati   Gujarat is a very old and a very important region for trade. Arab merchants had settled here in AD 916 and by 1315, agents of the Genoan bank of the Vivaldis had established factories (warehouses) in the area (Tirmizi, 1984: 60). Towards the end of the eighteenth century, the financial and merchant Bania[12] networks were concentrated in the great Mughal port of Surat. They spread across the Ganga valley all the way to Dhaka in Bengal and to South-East Asia, as well as to the ports of the Persian Gulf, West Asia and East Africa. After the collapse of the Mughal empire, it was the Banias who financed the East India Company in Bombay, as well as other local powers. At the end of the nineteenth century, having grown prosperous from

---

[12] The words 'bania' (or 'banya', 'vania') in northern India, and 'chettiar' (or 'chettyar', 'chettiyar') in southern India means 'merchant'.

domestic trade with the export firms of Calcutta and Bombay, they started textile industries in Ahmedabad and Bombay. Kasturbhai Lalbhai, founder of the great industrial group of Ahmedabad that still bears his name (Arvind Mills is the flagship company), descended from a certain Sheth Shantidas (c. 1590–1659) of the Oswal Jain community, who was sufficiently rich and influential to have direct access to the Mughal emperors and to advance them money (Tripathi, 1990: 88–9). H. Walchand, another great entrepreneur of Indian industry, came from a Gujarati Digamber Jain family settled in Sholapur in Maharashtra. Walchand created, before Independence, the first big maritime company with Indian capital, as also the firm Premier Automobiles. Besides the Hindu Banias (Meshri) and the Jain Banias (Shravak), many Gujarati communities of less importance took to trade and industrial activities. Thus the Charotar region of Kheda district, south of mainland Gujarat, is the native land of the Kunbi–Patidar or Patel peasants, who took to trade and industry around the turn of the nineteenth century. Mostly followers of the Swaminarayan sect (which has constructed a massive temple in London), the Patels migrated to Africa and, from there, to the United Kingdom and to the United States. In the USA they are famous for their motels (popularly called 'Motel-Patel'!). In India, K. Patel started Nirma, an important Ahmedabad firm that manufacturers detergents and soaps. But generally speaking, after Independence, the Gujarati business groups lost the importance that they once had. The only exception is the Ambanis, although they are not from a traditional merchant caste, and their Reliance Group of Industries (see Chapter II), which had the largest turnover in India in 1999–2000.

The Parsi community became an economic force in Bombay during the colonial period. Many migrated abroad at the time of Independence, especially to America. Numbering a mere one million in 1961 (Kulke, 1978), they founded several big industrial groups, of which the Godrej, Wadia, and Tata groups are notable. Zoroastrians from Persia, they fled from religious persecution to Gujarat in India in 697 (Desai, 1992: 99–108), and took to agriculture. In the fourteenth century they settled in the Surat and Navsari regions, where, along with agriculture, they practised trade, tax-farming, shipbuilding, and maritime

Parsi

freight. In 1735, after having ordered a certain Dhunjibhoy to build a ship, the East India Company charged one of its foremen, Lowjee Nusserwanji, to construct dockyards in Bombay. These became the Mazagaon Docks, where more than 350 ships were built. The Parsis moved from Surat–Navsari to Bombay, where a large percentage of their community had already settled in the eighteenth century (Guha, 1984: 109–50). Here they started trading with the Persian Gulf countries, and exporting cotton and opium to China. Those who remained in Surat–Navsari chose not to get into industry in any major way, but manufactured and exported silk and cotton cloth. The Bombay Parsis maintained excellent relations with the British, for whom they acted as middlemen. The pioneers of the Bombay textile industry are mostly descended from these Parsi merchants, ship-owners and financiers. Cowasji Nanabhoy Daver, the son of a rich merchant and a financier and exporter of cotton in his own right, founded the first Indian spinning and weaving mill, opened three banks and set up the first hydraulic press in Bombay. The Petits, Wadias and above all the Tatas, built industrial empires. Born to a family of Zoroastrian priests from Navsari, who had migrated to Bombay, Jamshet N. Tata (1839–1904) founded the group that still bears his name. Its flagship companies are Tata Iron and Steel Company (TISCO) which produces steel in Jamshedpur (Bihar), and the Tata Engineering Locomotive Company (TELCO) which manufactures trucks and buses in Pune (Maharashtra). The Tata group appears to be more Westernized than the other large Indian groups. Well known for its able management and quality products, it today often competes with the Birlas for first place among the industrial groups (see Chapter II).

Punjabi   The principal merchant castes of the Punjab are the Khatris, Aroras and Agarwals.[13] Each of these merchant castes comprises a Sikh section (Grewal, 1984: 186–209). Already known in the fifteenth century, the Khatris were trading in the seventeenth and eighteenth centuries in Afghanistan, Iran and Russia (starting from Astrakhan, and moving along the Volga to Moscow), and with the Khanats in Uzbekistan. Their networks

[13] Also called Agrawal, Aggarwal, etc.

linked Delhi, Multan, Lahore and later Amritsar. When the 1911 census was taken, the Khatris were predominant in Lahore, the Aroras in Multan and the Agarwals in Delhi. Towards 1921, the Khatris were already controlling some 300 industrial establishments and the Aroras around 50. At the time of Partition several Hindu industrialists moved from the Pakistan side of the Punjab to the Indian side, where they re-established their enterprises. Among them were the Munjals, who set up the Hero group (bicycles and two-wheelers) in Ludhiana, and the Nandas the Escorts group (tractors). The Ranbaxy pharmaceuticals group is on the way to becoming one of the first Indian multinationals in its speciality. The proximity of Pakistan has prevented the industrial development of certain sectors, and a large section of the mechanical industries in the Punjab still has many small and medium sized enterprises.

Spread across Gujarat, Bombay and Maharashtra, the Lohanas and Bhatias came to Kutch and Saurashtra (or Kathiawar) well before the partition of Sindh in 1947. In the eighteenth century, from the port of Mandvi (Kutch), the Bhatias traded in cotton, cloth and foodgrains with Bombay, the Malabar coast, Muscat, the Persian Gulf countries, and Arabia. The Khatau Bhatias entered the textile industry in Bombay before 1880. The Lohanas controlled a considerable share of the Ugandan cotton industry before being expelled in 1972. The Somaiya group (sugar, salt, chemicals, etc.), is one of the most important business houses established by them. The word 'Sindhi' designates an Indian Hindu refugee who left Sindh (Pakistan) at the time of Partition in 1947. Today spread across more than 150 countries, they are mainly descended from a group of Hyderabad (Sindh) merchants who, in the second half of the nineteenth century, began to trade in handicrafts. They initially sold their wares in Bombay, then moved to West Asia and to East and South-East Asia, where they finally settled and set up large firms. Many Sindhis who had come to India in 1947, restarted different businesses, in particular in the Bombay–Ulhasnagar area. Hinduja (with assets worth one billion pounds sterling) is the most important Sindhi firm. Its headquarters are in London and, in India, it controls Ashok Leyland. The Hindujas also have business interests in Nigeria. The Sindhis

*Lohana,
Bhatia
and
Sindhi*

tend to view themselves as highly Westernized, while maintaining a strong sense of their own culture. Numbering over two million individuals in India and one million abroad, they constitute a business community that has continued to grow over the past century.

MERCHANT CASTES AND COMMUNITIES OF SOUTH INDIA

Nagarattar   Among the different Chettiar merchant castes, the Nagarattar or Nattukottai Chettiars from Chetty-Nad, Tamil Nadu, are the most prominent today. In the seventeenth century they were petty itinerant merchants. A century later they were trading in rice, cloth, arrack, silver, and their financial networks spread from Calcutta to Ceylon. In the nineteenth and at the beginning of the twentieth centuries, the Nagarattar bankers became one of the principal sources of credit in South-East Asia. They financed tea and coffee cultivation and trade in Ceylon, rice in Burma, as well as rubber plantations and tin mines in Malaysia. In French Indochina, they competed with Chinese money-lenders. In the Madras Presidency, the big Nagarattar money-lenders seized their bankrupt debtors' lands and got the titles registered in their names. They founded great institutions (such as the Annamalai University of Chidambaram) and constructed beautiful palatial residences in their native villages. During the first few decades of the twentieth century the Nagarattar élite progressively transferred their capital from trade to industry. But it was really after Independence that they set up the industrial groups that rank among the first in India today—the most important being the M.A. Chidambaram (MAC) and Murugappan groups.

Kamma Naidu   Originally from Andhra Pradesh, the Kamma Naidus, cotton planters from the Coimbatore area, opened spinning and weaving mills between the two world wars (the Lakshmi group). They contributed considerably to the development of Coimbatore, which has become one of the major industrial centres of Tamil Nadu. They are also very active today in Vishakhaptnam, a big port and industrial centre of Andhra Pradesh.

The Hindu Nadars (there are also Christians) are among those *Nadar*
merchant castes that are gaining in importance since the end of
the 1960s. Natives of south Tamil Nadu, where their traditional
occupation was collecting palm juice, the Nadars transformed
Sivakasi into the biggest centre for the manufacture of matches,
fireworks and printing. The Nadars established Tuticorin Mills
Ltd. and Hindustan Computers Ltd. They recently lost control
of the Tamilnadu Mercantile Bank Ltd., which was their
community bank.

BRAHMINS, MUSLIMS, CHRISTIANS AND JEWS

Although their traditional vocation was a sacerdotal one, there *Brahmins*
was no dearth of traders or financiers, and even soldiers and
politicians among the Brahmins. For the purpose of this study
we shall treat them as a group, but in reality the numerous
castes to which they belong have little in common with each
other. The Gaud Saraswat Brahmins from Mangalore in Karna-
taka, have largely contributed to the creation of several banks
of which four are today part of the nineteen nationalized banks
(Thingalaya, 1999). The shares of many of these banks were
reserved for members of the founder's caste. The Karhada
Kirloskar Brahmins of Maharashtra founded an important group
of mechanical industries that produce diesel motors, generators,
pumps, etc. Most new entrepreneurs in the mechanical industries' sector based in Pune, often also from the local Brahmin
castes, consider them exemplary leaders. Together with the
Pune-based Tata and Bajaj enterprises, the Kirloskars have
greatly contributed to making Pune the second most important
industrial city of Maharashtra after Bombay. In the 1960s, a
Brahmin group from Tamil Nadu, T.V. Sundaram Iyengar,
developed its activities in the field of automobile parts and
components, and in the 1980s, diversified into the manufacture
of durable consumer goods (motorcycles, washing machines,
etc.). After the division of the family in 1993, the group's assets
were separated into three divisions, of which the most important remains TVS (870 crores, or a turnover of Rs. 8.7 billion in
1995-6). Many Iyer Brahmin industrialists come from Kalla-
daikurichi, near Tirunelveli.

Muslims   The Bohra and Khoja Shia Ismaili Muslim communities and
the Sunni Memon community came into being through the
conversion of Gujarati and Sindhi Hindus to Islam in the
fifteenth century (Engineer, 1989). At the time of Independence, the greater part of their élite moved to Pakistan,
where the Memons did very well and became big industrialists (Papanek, 1973). These three communities have a strong
presence in East and South Africa, and the Bohras are particularly prominent in Madagascar. The Indian groups Wipro
(information technology) and Cipla (pharmaceuticals) were
started by the Bohras. South Indian Muslims find a mention in
the literature of the eighth century. The Kerala Muslims were
called Mappila (or Moplah), and those of Tamil Nadu Marak-
kayar, Rawther, and Labbai. The latter, once doing considerable
trade with South-East Asia, today control the major part of the
leather industry in Tamil Nadu (see Chapter III).

Christians   The St. Thomas Christians are supposed to have come from
Syria in AD 52–4. The Syrian Catholic Bank Ltd. has a well-
known network in south India, and the MRF group is an
important manufacturer of tyres. Armenian merchants have
been in India since the Mughal period (Meshrovb, 1983). At
the beginning of the eighteenth century, Iranian Armenians
settled in Bengal, and later in Bombay and Madras, where their
churches still exist. They migrated to the West at the time of
Independence.

Jews   Settled in Kerala, the Cochin Jewish merchants collaborated
with the Dutch. In the nineteenth century, other Jews from
Baghdad, the best known of whom is the magnate David
Sassoon, owned several weaving mills in Bombay. A little before
Independence, the Baghdadi Jews migrated to Great Britain,
the United States and Australia.

CASTES AND MAJOR BUSINESS HOUSES

Business   It seems that business circles are not always indifferent to the
Houses   social origins of the biggest among them. Thus, in 1996 the
magazine *Marwar*, published by the Marwari community, came
out with an honours list of Indian communities that had

established the largest industrial firms.[14] It was clear that, on the basis of their overall turnover, the Marwaris were well in the lead. They were followed by the Parsis, Gujaratis, Punjabis, groups from south India, the Sindhis, an independent Muslim businessman, and other unclassified groups. Although an approximation, these results correspond to the financial analyses made by other scholars (Dutta, 1997: 124–37). In 1997, the magazine *Business Today*[15] published for the first time in thirty years a carefully compiled classification of the 100 biggest Indian family-owned business houses ('business houses' and not companies). This classification and the detailed notes on the fifty biggest ones were established on the basis of data pertaining to the year 1995–6 (see Appendices 1 and 2).

In 1995–6, the Parsi group Tata was leading the field with a turnover of more than Rs. 30,000 crores (Rs. 300 billion). It was followed by the Marwari group of B.K. and K.M. Birla with a turnover of around 11,000 crores. The Gujarati group, Ambani, came third with 8,468 crores. Next on the list was the Marwari group of R.P. Goenka with 5,641 cores. Groups that were fifth to twenty-fourth in rank had a turnover between Rs. 5,000 and 2,000 crores, and the last forty groups in the listing had a turnover between 1,000 and 500 crores. From the biggest to the smallest among the first 100 groups, the difference was of 60 to 1; the small to medium-sized groups were greater in number. In the organized large-scale industries sector, the share of private family-owned enterprises was 25 per cent of total sales, 32 per cent of the profits after taxes, 18 per cent of the fixed assets, and 37 per cent of the reserves. The big business houses showed a satisfactory growth despite the restrictions and other measures to which they were subjected. The community-wise distribution that we have attempted here for the first fifty enterprises[16] (see Table 2, and Appendix 2 for more details), confirms that the Marwaris are more numerous, and that together they have the biggest turnover. The Gujaratis and the

Turnover

---

[14] Gita Piramal (1996: 91–7). The data given in the table was taken from the classification of the big companies and business houses realized by *Business India Super* 100 (23 October 1995).

[15] *Business Today*, 1997: the results are given on pages 220–7, and the method of analysis and calculation is described in detail on page 217.

[16] Based on table in *Business Today*, 1997.

TABLE 2: TURNOVER BY COMMUNITY (1995–6)

	Groups		Global Turnover	
	Number	Rank	Rupees (crore)	Rank
Marwari	19	1	51,399	1
Punjabi	7–8	2	18,161	3
Gujarati	5–6	3	16,915	4
Parsi	3	4	35,463	2
Chettiar	2	5	6,367	5
Brahmin	2–3	6	6,172	6
Sindhi	2	7	4,523	7
Christian	1	8	2,011	9
Nair	1	8	2,148	8
Raju	1	8	1,341	10
Muslim	1	8	1,287	11
Unidentified	3	–	5,106	–
Total	49–52		150,893	

Note: This community-wise classification is a very approximate one. The Marwaris comprise several subdivisions (the Birlas are from the Maheshwari subdivision), and the denomination Punjabi refers to the most representative merchant castes (Khatri, Arora, Agarwal), of which some are originally from Marwar. There are numerous Gujarati merchant castes. The two Chettiar groups are subdivisions of the well-known Nagarattar bankers. The Nambiars of the BPL group are Nairs (farmers, soldiers, traders) from Kerala.

Punjabis are more or less equal, both with regard to the number of groups as well as their global turnover. The Parsi groups, of which Tata is by far the most important, are few.

Head-quarters The headquarters of the fifty most important groups are situated in the big Indian metropolises: 14 in Bombay, 14 in Delhi, 8 in Calcutta, 5 in Madras, and in some of the state capitals: 3 in Bangalore, 2 in Ahmedabad, 2 in Pune and 1 each in Hyderabad and Indore (the B.K.–K.M. Birla, and G.P.–C.K. Birla groups have two headquarters each, one in Calcutta, the other in Bombay and in Delhi). The headquarters of the two Sindhi groups are abroad, the Hindujas in London, and M.R. Chhabria in Dubai (which no doubt reflects the highly dia-sporic character of the Sindhi community).

Divisions and Alliances If certain families had not separated, notes *Business Today* (1997), their groups would have had a better ranking. The five branches of the Birla group of the 1980s would together have a consolidated turnover of Rs. 20,320 crores, the two Goenka branches would have been Rs. 8,082 crores, etc. From 1952 to 1997, thirty-nine undivided industrial families separated (*Business Today*, 1998: 45–6). But many of them are also connected through marriage. The biographer of Lakshmipat Singhania, from the Marwari J.K. Singhania group (which would have been sixth of fifty had the family not separated in 1979, and again in 1992), remarks: 'In India as elsewhere, it is not uncommon for wealth to wed wealth. The spouses of the sons [of L. Singhania] have hailed from the well-known Business Houses of Ruias and Vaids of Bombay, Agarwals of Kanpur and Dagas of Calcutta, and the daughters were married into equally well-known families of Jains of Bombay, Pittis of Hyderabad, Jhunjhunwalas of Kanpur and Agarwals of Calcutta' (Chentsal, 1986: 58). The Ruias, Agarwals, Jhunjhunwalas are well-known Marwari business families, and some of them figure among the fifty most important groups. L. Singhania was not indifferent to his community, and when still young, was selected to preside at the meeting of the All-India Marwari Federation in Kanpur in 1940, during which he appealed to his brothers to work for the country (Chentsal, 1986: 101–3).

Ever since the mid-nineteenth century (when India climbed on to the industrialization bandwagon), the majority of business houses in India trace their origin to merchant castes and communities, excluding the British groups of which the biggest after Independence was Hindustan Lever. Some analysts point out that the community origins of today's industrialists tend to diversify, signifying by that that they are neither Parsi, nor Marwari, nor Gujarati (Piramal, 2000: 34–5). This may be true, but they nevertheless often come from well-known business communities: those with a merchant vocation who have only recently turned to industry (Sindhis, Bohras), or agrarian landowning classes who have been in the process of social mobility over the past century (the Kamma Naidus), or the traditionally-educated classes (Brahmins) who have always favoured the professions (including trade and finance). The difference is that now the new big entrepreneurs tap the stock market for their capital requirements (Ambani, Infosys Technologies), get professionals to manage their business (Ranbaxy), and probably feel less tied to their community of origin.

*Diversi-
fication*

VALUE-CONCEPTS

Traditions ('Great' and 'Little')

Contemporary Indian culture is composed of more or less ancient sedimentary layers, to which various influences from Europe came to be added from the eighteenth century onwards. The relationship between the 'Great Tradition' (Brahmanic, Jain or Buddhist educated thinking) and the popular representations and behaviour of the 'Little Tradition' do not resemble those found in European societies. In India there is often a deep interpenetration of the two: mythology, for example, can serve as the substratum for intense philosophical speculation, and this in turn may go hand-in-hand with popular cults. Nor was there a serious differentiation between 'theory' and 'practice' as the philosophical autobiography of Gandhi illustrates, where, describing his 'Experiments with Truth', he continuously refers to his dietetic and sexual problems, style of dressing, or his grocery accounts. ... At the same time he refers to the joys he experienced in his encounters with truth, *satya*, the True and the Real, that is to say an aspect of what he considers the ultimate reality (Gandhi, 1982). By first placing oneself in time and space, all reflection apprehends and conceives the relationships between things, between men, between men and the universe. We therefore begin with concrete examples of some of these basic relationships and categories with the help of facts and rituals of professional life that are part of the Little Tradition. We then evoke the principal concepts of the Great Tradition that the neo-Hindu reformers of the nineteenth century helped to popularize. Lastly, we show how management specialists endeavour to use these concepts to develop a Hindu doctrine of work motivation.

THE 'LITTLE TRADITION': EVERYDAY LIFE

Compartmentalization

In his study of Madras industrialists conducted in the 1960s, Singer observed, as many after him, that they had adapted to the demands of modern life by 'compartmentalizing' their everyday life (Singer, 1996: 438–9). The separation between the place of work and the home, a commonplace phenomenon in urban areas, led to the creation of two separate spheres of behaviour and corresponding norms. The place of residence fell into the realm of religious and time-honoured values, in which the relationship and conduct towards one's kin and caste, predominated. The office and the factory on the contrary, fell into the realm of business and modern life, where relationships of the universal type were forged. Western clothes rather than the *dhoti* or the *lungi* were worn, English rather than the mother tongue was spoken. One ate uncustomary dishes in the canteen or in the restaurant with colleagues of different castes with whom the conversation touched upon work-related matters. Once at home, one changed one's clothes, took a purifying not just hygienic bath, isolated oneself an instant to meditate in the prayer room (puja room), and took meals, served by the women who ate later, on a metal platter without any cutlery. Afterwards no tobacco or alcohol was taken, but a betel leaf was enjoyed, and the strategy to be employed for the marriage of a sister discussed with younger brothers. In this example, the coexistence of frequently incompatible norms and behaviour is facilitated by their spatial and temporal separation. But in many spheres of psychological, social and political life, this separation is more difficult to put into practice. Thus, one advocates love marriages, but when it comes to one's own children arranged marriages are preferred, one bemoans caste prejudice but nevertheless unconsciously practises it, and the discourse of numerous politicians is an amalgamation of concepts from antagonistic doctrines. Contextual separation and amalgamation are two of the more common modes of acculturation, that moreover, Westerners residing in India end up by adopting, if only in their food habits.

Calendars

Philosophical–religious discourses or even commonplace ones refer to eras or *yugas*, of classical Brahmanic cosmogony. Of unequal duration, *yugas* succeed one another indefinitely, going progressively down the scale from the best to the worst, within a human society which is in a state of degeneracy.[17] India officially adopted the Gregorian calendar in 1947. But in their day-to-day life, Indians use several other calendars according to

[17] The first *yuga* is the longest (17,28,000 years) and was supposed to be the golden age. We are living in the fourth, called *kaliyuga*, which is the worst.

their region or religion.[18] The year is subdivided into six seasons
and twelve lunar months (plus an intercalary month), with two
dark and light fortnights corresponding to the moon's waxing
and waning phases. The days, noted after the readings of the
sun and the moon, come under the influence of the twelve
zodiacal sun constellations, and the twenty-seven or -eight lunar
houses (*nakshatra*). These different calendars govern the domestic and ritual life of all social classes. Astrologers cast the
horoscopes of newly-engaged couples, and advise politicians
and businessmen. An auspicious day and hour are chosen to
initiate or conclude a new business venture, to inaugurate a
house, to make a wish, or to marry. Agendas and almanacs
(*panchang*) in the vernacular languages indicate precisely the
good and bad moments of the day. Thus, the calendar adopted
by a merchant community under the heading 'Auspicious
moments to take out the ledgers and place orders', recommends
the worship (puja) of money in one's house on Friday, the
thirteenth day of the waning moon in the month of *Ashvin* (5-
11-99), in the morning from 8.07 a.m. to 10.50 a.m., or in the
evening from 4.45 p.m. to 6 p.m., or at night from 9.15 p.m. to
10.15 p.m.[19] One is reminded that it is befitting to display the
cushion (*gaddi*) representing the headquarters of the firm, and
to take out the ledgers. On occasion, a businessman will
graciously give a copy of his particular calendar to those with
whom he has dealings. Whatever the calendar system adopted,
time is not experienced or conceived in linear progression of
undifferentiated moments that would add arithmetically one to
the other. Human time is a part of cosmic time, which has
important qualitative properties influencing everyday behaviour.

Vastushastra   Whether offices or factories, the work place is decorated with
statues of gods and saints and gurus, which are generally
indicative of the religious or sectarian affiliation of the chief
occupant. The latter usually begins his day by lighting perfumed
incense sticks (*agarbatti*), and offering some flowers with a short
prayer. It is moreover not uncommon to find a temple in the

----

[18] The Muslim calendar starts with the Hegira in AD 622, and the Jain in
527 BC. The two most common Hindu calendars refer either to the Shaka
era (AD 78–9) or to the Samvat era (57 BC).

[19] This does not refer to Lakshmi puja (see below).

courtyard of a factory, or even on the upper floors of high-rise buildings of the big Bombay firms. Constructed for the convenience of office personnel, these temples are incorporated in the firm's assets, and it has been suggested that they be included among the depreciable items in the company's inventory (*Business India*, 1997). They might be dedicated to a pan-Indian god like Ganesh, or for example, to Vishvakarma, the patron of artisans, labourers and architects. Monuments, places of worship, and even towns are built according to the guiding principles that take into account certain telluric influences and the good or bad qualities connected with their orientation. In fact whether it be the construction of a house or an industrial building, work begins only after the *Bhoomipuja*, a ritual conducted at a propitious time to ward off evil influences. Architectural techniques and geomantic knowledge for a construction in harmony with the universe, are specified in ancient treatises (*Vastushastra*[20]) which, in the past decade, have been modified to suit changing tastes. Some of these recent publications specialize in non-religious contemporary architecture (Chakrabarti, 1999). The auspicious orientation of a building and its inauguration also at the auspicious time, contribute to its harmonious positioning in a universe where macrocosm and microcosm are linked by clusters of symbolic correspondences. Man is not confronted with a coldly objectified universe, but exists in cosmic space–time. The revival of this *Vastu* tradition induces one to believe that there is today a greater integration of the work place with the all-encompassing sphere of religion. But had it ever been left out? At all events, sanitary norms have become an important ingredient in the construction of the work place, a concept that is foreign to the ancient *Vastushastra*.

In 1998, Maharishi Mahesh Yogi, the founder of Transcendental Meditation and the Maharishi University of Management,[21]

Maharishi

---

[20] These ancient scholarly treatises are part of the Great Tradition; we can see how awkward it is to separate the Great and the Little Traditions.

[21] MUM was established in the United States in 1971 and is recognized up to the doctorate level by the North Central Association of Colleges and Schools. It has created the Maharishi Institute of Management, which offers American MBA programmes in major Indian cities.

created a special fund of 550 million dollars in New York. He plans to issue Rs. 470 million worth of shares, (67 million FF) for the reconstruction of the major cities of the world according to the principles of *Vastushastra* (*Business World*, 1998).

Pollution and Purification

Some rituals were thought to have a positive influence on the physical world and the course of things. They have now disappeared or acquired a purely ceremonial and symbolic character. But sometimes one continues to use ritual when interacting with matter and the physical environment in order to guard against their potentially dangerous and harmful effects. During the Dussehra festival (September–October), work-tools are often worshipped (puja), in order to prevent accidents. For example, employees of a small printing press in Pondicherry squeeze a lemon filled with vermilion pigment over the dangerous parts of the machines in the presence of the manager who presides over the ritual. The red juice symbolizes blood offered preventively to the machines so that they do not spill the operator's blood. In 1986, an extremely toxic volatile gas leaked out in a Bhopal factory, causing over 2,000 deaths (N.K. Singh, 1986). Massive ceremonies were conducted at the site of the accident: 800 kg. of clarified butter, 1.5 tons of rice, several quintals of barley, and 375 kg. of sugar were burnt on the sacrificial altar. The Brahmin dignitary (*Swami*) who had organized the sacrifice (*yagna*) with the help of 500 pandits from all over India, affirmed that the ritual could improve the atmosphere and the environment, and even eliminate the radioactivity (of which there was no danger). A local paper demanded that all the industrialists in the state be directed to perform a purificatory ritual every year, and further suggested that they would be well advised to perform other rituals collectively in each city at the level of their federation. More-over, it was suggested that the *Swami* award a 'pollution-free' certificate, valid for at least one year. Death is generally the cause of ritual pollution, but in this case, ritual and chemical pollution were spontaneously amalgamated.

Lakshmi Puja

The Vaishya is only third in rank in the *varna* order, and economic matters are only the second of man's goals (see below p. 57, *Purushartha*). But there is nothing shameful in the desire for monetary gain in those whose vocation it is. In the world of business and industry, the puja or worship of the goddess of wealth, Lakshmi, is performed at the end of the ritual year, which coincides with the traditional financial year when accounts are closed. Astrologers fix the date and hour. The person who officiates is generally the *karta* of the firm or the enterprise, or a Brahmin. In small firms, the objects of worship and offerings are placed on the *karta's* table or chair, before a likeness of Lakshmi, with for example, Ganesh and Saraswati on either side.[22] Lakshmi is also represented by at least a silver or gold coin and other monetary symbols such as bank notes, chequebook, and even the key to the safe. The coin is washed in milk and treated in the manner as a temple idol. Then the new account books and ledgers, traditionally covered with an auspicious red cloth, are inaugurated. On the first page, in red ink, are inscribed the words *shubh* and *labh* (good fortune and profit), a *swastika* (a gammadion cross) and other auspicious symbols, followed by the names of Lakshmi, Ganesh, Saraswati, of the caste or ancestral deity (*kuldevata*), of the *karta's* guru, etc. The balance of the year ending is brought forward and inscribed in the new account books and ledgers and can also be worshipped (puja of the balance). Then on the debit side of the new accounts a symbolic sum representing a donation with a number ending in '1' (101, 1,001, etc.) is inscribed. Sometimes a supplier takes the initiative of charging his client a charity tax (*dharmadan*) which figures on his bills. The puja finished, the *prasad*[23] (edible offerings to the gods that are consecrated through puja) is distributed among the spectators and the partners or principal shareholders required to be present. Employees, or their representatives, are also given *prasad*, and above all a special bonus. The principal suppliers and clients receive gifts during the day, often a gold or silver coin symbolic of Lakshmi. Lakshmi puja is performed regularly by Hindus and Jains, sometimes even by Christians, each giving it the secondary interpretation that suits them. For the Brahmin, who

[22] Ganesh, the god with the elephant head, removes obstacles. He is often invoked before undertaking a difficult task, such as an examination. Saraswati is the goddess of the arts and of knowledge.

[23] The *prasad* which is distributed is the symbolic equivalent of a sacrificial victim; and puja is the vegetarian equivalent of a bloody sacrifice.

is paid by the *karta* for his services, all money must be purified before a donation.

Tirupati   Certain gods and goddesses may be considered auspicious partners or shareholders of a business, whose profits and dividends they share. The most famous example is that of Venkateshvara, the Vaishnavite divinity of the Tirupati temple in Andhra Pradesh. The Trust that manages the temple employs 7,500 people, who work in three eight-hour shifts to cater to the 30,000 pilgrims who come every day to worship the divinity. One of them is the Marwari industrialist, R.P. Goenka, who goes at the beginning of each year to Tirupati with his family to 'see' (*darshan*) Lord Venkateshvara, of whom he has the honour of being one of the administrators. Goenka employs some 71 Brahmins who pray daily for him and for the success of his business. He offers puja every day and also organizes a big *yagna* each year in the garden of his Delhi house (Piramal, 1996 : 245–6). In 1983, various forms of wealth were deposited in Venkateshvara's *hundi* (trunk), including a gold crown weighing 300 gm, thirty cheques worth Rs. 1.05 million; a Maruti car was also offered. Many devotees, including Muslims and Christians, come also from abroad and give foreign exchange. In 1984, the temple revenues totalled some 3,365 crores (Rs. 33.65 billion), which made it the richest temple in India (*Business India*, 1984). The Vice-President of the Trust was then also the Chief Minister of Andhra Pradesh. His wish was to turn Tirupati into the 'Vatican' of India, whose CEO would be Lord Venkateshvara himself. Perhaps because in contemporary Indian law, Hindu idols are a legal entity (Annussamy, 1991).

Seva and Philanthropy   Commemorative inscriptions in the oldest Indian temples testify to the generosity of devotees, princes, merchants, guilds and other institutions. Religious donations and service (*seva*) of the divinity were no doubt very important for the salvation of the donor merchant, but they also served to enhance his economic standing and his reputation, the two being inextricably linked (Haynes, 1987). Moreover, the prestige of the great and pious merchant reflected upon his community, after which it was more inclined to recognize him as its leader and representative *vis-à-vis* the political authorities. In the colonial era, these big merchants, and after them the industrialists, began to finance secular philanthropic works, without however stopping their religious donations. After Independence, the industrialist's and his family's prestige continued to contribute to their economic credit. As S.L. Kirloskar put it (arguing in favour of family-run businesses but without mentioning donations), 'This has been a very important factor in rehabilitating and establishing many companies. In many cases . . . the owning family's reputation has a beneficial influence on the financial institutions to get assistance. They feel that the reputation of the family is at stake, and therefore the unit will be managed properly' (Lachaier, 1999: 183). And there is not one biography of an industrialist or a merchant today that has not devoted some pages to his philanthropic works (improvements to the city of Pune by Kirloskar, hospital by the Hindujas in Bombay), as well as any religious foundations he may have established (the Shri Lakshminarayan temple by the Birlas in Delhi, the Shri Radhakrishna temple by the Singhanias in Kanpur, etc.). Today sponsorship is added to *seva* and philanthropy, without however replacing them.

THE 'GREAT TRADITION':
CLASSICAL IDEAS AND VALUES

The great classics have amply commented upon the cardinal Brahmanical virtues, or 'The goals of man' (*Purushartha*). They are generally presented in the form of a hierarchic series of 4 or 3+1 terms: *dharma, artha, kama/moksha*. The last term—*moksha*—concerns particularly those who have renounced worldly life and are single-mindedly pursuing salvation. The second (*artha*) is the political function of the Kshatriya. The third—*kama*—refers to all pleasure and enjoyment and especially the pleasures of the flesh. The numerous contemporary editions of the work on the subject, the *Kamasutras*, have contributed in popularizing this concept. As for the classical treatises on *dharma* (order, duty), they continue to inspire juridical texts in India to date.[24]

Goals of Man

---

[24] The principal treatise on *dharma* is written by Manu.

Dharma

Dharma is the cosmic, social and moral law or order. It also signifies 'duty', 'obligation' in the general sense. But each community (*varna*, caste or *jati*) contributes to the global social order through the pursuit of its particular vocation or duty, i.e. by pursuing its *swadharma*. Thus, the study of the classics and a vegetarian regimen are in conformity with the vocation (or *swadharma*) of the Brahmin, whereas war-related activities and a meat-eating regimen suit the Kshatriya temperament; the former must abstain from all violent behaviour, but the latter can legitimately shed blood. Jains and Hindus who consider themselves part of the third *varna*, are vegetarians and have chosen a non-violent pattern of behaviour (*ahimsa*). Such is the case with the merchants and industrialists from the Bania castes of Gujarat, of whom Mahatma Gandhi is one of the most notable examples.[25] The concept of *swadharma* can also apply to the family, religious or worldly obligations of the individual.

Artha

Artha deals in particular with the material advantages ensuing from the Kshatriya's political function. Treatises on *artha* teach in a very concrete and non-euphemistic manner, how to govern in order to preserve the social order, that is to say *dharma*, and what military and economic means need to be mobilized for this. *Artha* is also concerned with money, profit, and manu-facturing and commercial activities. Let us emphasize that the economic sphere was not conceived independently of politics, to which it is subordinated. The most famous treatise on *artha* is that of Kautilya (Shamashastry, 1967). It is referred to or studied in certain seminars especially designed for business executives and managerial staff.

Moksha

Moksha is the highest of man's goals and concerns each one individually. It means salvation, absolute freedom, and can be understood in several non-exclusive ways. On the one hand man attempts to free himself from the infinite cycles of birth and rebirth (*samsara*) to which he is subjected according to the law of retribution for one's actions, or the law of *karma*: physical and psychic actions, good or bad, have cumulative effects whose balance sheet conditions a man's status in a future reincarnation.

---

[25] M.K. Gandhi was the son of a minister of the princely state of Porbandar, Kathiawar. The Gandhis are relatively strict Modh Banias.

One the other hand, *moksha* can be understood as the final goal of a spiritual evolution that endeavours to generate awareness of the ultimate Reality. The great revelations, the Upanishads in particular, state that the entity or the supreme cosmic consciousness, the Brahman, universal and unique, is also present inside each human being as *atman*. The Hindu can attain *moksha* by reaching a higher state of consciousness in which he can achieve the oneness of his *atman* with the Brahman. Whether they are implicit or more or less rationalized and refined, the notions of *karma*, *samsara* and *moksha* are common to all Hindus, Jains and Buddhists, who in fact have their own interpretations (*nirvana* is the Buddhist equivalent of *moksha*).

On the one hand, the schools and systems of philosophico-religious thought—classical or contemporary—may well be mutually incompatible, but are considered as legitimate points of view (*darshana*) on what is Brahman. On the other, the diverse tangible forms of the divine which are worshipped are also legitimate, in the sense that they represent aspects of the supreme being. In other words, whether it is at the level of texts or of custom, each one can chose the divine representation he desires, and adopt the path and specific practices that lead to *moksha*. [26] One can thus be a Vaishnavite or a Shivaite, a Sikh, a Jain or a Buddhist, and agree in principle that Zoroastra, Jesus and Mohammad are sages who found authentic and original paths to salvation and Brahman. The great reformers and Hindu thinkers have stressed this all-encompassing trait of Hinduism in order to promote it to the rank of 'Religion of Religions', or 'the Eternal Religion' (Sanatana Dharma). Nonetheless, in contemporary neo-Hinduism, the best known of the great paths to salvation (*marg* or *yoga*) remains that of knowledge (*jnanamarg*), devotion (*bhaktimarg*), and action (*karmamarg*) (Vivekananda, 1972). They are more or less complementary and non-exclusive. The path of knowledge is that of metaphysical and philosophical reflection. That of devotion extols the devotee's love for the divinity, which he glorifies in his prayers, songs, etc.; it is most widespread among the merchants of north

Paths to Salvation

[26] Gandhi's autobiography is an account of the 'practico-spiritual' process leading to *moksha*.

India. The path of action, which in ancient times was that of sacrificial action, is eulogized in the *Bhagavad Gita*, the 'Song of the Lord',[27] and has recently become the preferred path of the entrepreneur and of the industrial world. The *Bhagavad Gita* simulates the dialogue between Arjun and his charioteer, Krishna, on the battlefield, where two related clans are confronting each other. Arjun is reluctant to take up arms against his cousins, but Krishna, recalling him to his duty (*swadharma*), gradually reveals his true identity as an avatar of Vishnu, and develops the doctrine of action without the fruit of action (*nishkam karma*), that is to say without *karmic* effect.

Action without Fruit of Action

Whether one be prince, weaver or shoemaker, whoever fulfils his duty (*swadharma*) without seeking a reward, will attain salvation. Different people have given different renderings of the passage in the *Bhagavad Gita* that best summarizes the doctrine of action. Gandhi noted in his autobiography (Gandhi, 1982: 339): 'I also realized that . . . I had disobeyed the essential principle of the *Gita*—namely that it is the duty of every man in a perfect state of harmony, to act without desire that the fruit of his action may arouse in him'. In one of the last notes that the great industrialist L. Singhania (1910–76) had written before his death, we also find several references to this passage in the *Gita*: 'To action alone hast thou a right and never at all to its fruit, let not the fruits of action be thy motive; neither let there be in thee any attachment to inaction' (Chentsal, 1986: 62–3). And Gujar Mal Modi (1902–76), founder of the industrial group that bears his name, was a true '*Karmayogi*', according to his employees in a commemorative address where the *Gita* is quoted: 'You have a right to perform your prescribed duty, but you are not entitled to the fruits of action. Never consider your self to be the cause of the results of your activities and never be attached to not doing your duty' (Lachaier, 1999, photo 6). It transpires that interpretations revolve around the same theme, action without the fruits of action, while continuing to emphasize individual concerns. For Gandhi, man must be in a state of internal harmony in order to accomplish

[27] The *Bhagavad Gita*, a chapter in the great epic of *Mahabharata*, is the best known and most commented upon text of contemporary Hinduism (Aurobindo, 1970).

acts without being motivated by the rewards as indicated in the *Bhagavad Gita*. As a more pragmatic man of action, Singhania's citation affirms the right (and not the duty) to action without consideration of its fruits, in other words disinterested action, and the duty never to become complaisant in non-action. The citation given by the Modi employees is closer to the original: the results of an act are in the last analysis not the effects of the human actor (of the 'self'), but rather that of the 'Self', that is to say of the divine that inhabits man in the form of *atman*, who must not be swayed from his natural duty (from his *swadharma*), in this case, the entrepreneurial calling that was Modi's.

The doctrine of action as expounded in the *Bhagavad Gita* was easy to re-interpret. Two great Hindu reformers, Aurobindo and Gandhi, experimented and constructed systems of thought and action that are close to the paths of salvation as described in the *Gita*. Aurobindo by integrating the theory of evolution (man is born of matter and evolves into a spiritual being), and Gandhi by applying the notions of non-violence (*ahimsa*) and action without the fruits thereof, to political activism. After Independence, the reformers, more concerned with socio-economic development (Agarwal, 1993: 3–260), strove to invent new techniques of work motivation which they tried to implement and experiment with in the industrial milieu. Such was the case with the Pune-based educational association Jnana Prabhodini (JP), which created several small and medium-sized industries with the help of prominent industrialists such as Kirloskar, Birla, Bajaj and Tata (Lachaier, 1999: 263–80). For JP, economic activities, although they have their own finality, are firstly conceived as a service, *seva*, rendered to society and to the Indian nation in particular. In this sense, they can be considered acts of religious merit. The JP workshops are likened to a 'Temple of Machines' (*Yantra-Mandir*), which the great industrialists are asked to bless: 'Shri Jamshetji Tata, Shri Walchand Hirachand, Shri Lakshmanrao Kirloskar . . ., Captains of industry, Bringing to Bharat the New Age of Technology (*Yantra-yuga*), Let their kindly gaze and benediction rest upon this *Yantra-Mandir*.' Prayers and rites accompany the daily tasks conceived as a sacrificial act leading to salvation: 'Work is worship', they say, to summarize the *Gita's* doctrine.

Work is Worship

Chakraborty S.K. Chakraborty is a man of many talents: a university professor, a professional consultant, a theoretician and a practitioner of management. Subsidized by the firm Escorts and published in 1987 by Tata Press and McGraw-Hill Publishing, Chakraborty's book, *Managerial Effectiveness and Quality of Work Life, Indian Insights*, received the DMA Escorts Award in 1988 (Lachaier, 1993: 56–63). The author achieved a bigger success with *Management with Values: Towards Cultural Congruence* published in 1991 by Oxford University Press, and reprinted in 1992. His work found its élan in his refusal to import techniques of motivation that, he felt, showed a tendency to treat man like a bundle of material needs and desires. The West of today, he says, manifests a basic incapacity to integrate all the dimensions of man at work, in particular spirituality (Chakraborty, 1987). The techniques of motivation suitable for Indians must rest on a sense of debt, obligation and giving. Not the right to have one's needs satisfied, with its model of corresponding needs (*Needing Model*),[28] but a sense of social duty and the need to give (*Giving Model*). Chakraborty gives a vivid and clear account of the doctrine of work without the fruit thereof (Chakraborty, 1995). It should not be understood as a call to pray on Sunday and work during the week (*Work and Workship*), nor as a proposal to work in the manner one prays (*Work as Worship*), but to treat one's work as an act of worship (*Work is Worship*) offered to the Supreme Energy (*Shakti*, an aspect of the Absolute). He is against the neo-liberal economic doctrines (*hedonomics* = hedonism + economics) and the socialist doctrines (*communomics* = communism + economics). In their stead, he proposes what he calls *Spironomics* (spirituality + economics) which draws its inspiration from the post-Vedic writings (*Upanishads*) and classic Indian values (Chakraborty, 1995): the goals of man (*purushartha*), the path of action (*karmayoga*), and the doctrine of work without the fruit thereof (*nishkam karma*). The reversal of values advocated by the author would mean giving primacy to the group over the individual, at the same time allowing the individual to devote himself to his personal salvation.

---

[28] The 'Needing Model' (or, if one wants to be ironic, the 'Model of Want, Need, Indigence'), as opposed to the 'Giving Model'.

CONCLUSION

Unless we study large-sized aggregates, we cannot really understand the functioning of the Indian economy independently of the basic social relations underlying its principal institutions, the conceptions of which it is equally important to understand. Thus, whatever the changes observed, marriage strategies remain the prerogative of the older members of the family, and not that of the future couple. As for the more or less extended family, whether organizing principle of the enterprise or not, it remains an ideal, and as such, a value in itself. The different kinship systems correspond to differences in the regional languages, and their local variations to the differences in status and religious affiliations; they help in the formation of communal identities.

Castes have given rise to numerous controversies amongst historians and sociologists, some have accorded them primary importance, others have predicted their disappearance in the near future, and yet others have denied their existence or gone to the extent of pretending they were a British invention. In an attempt to limit the controversies to known and proven facts, the last work on the subject concludes (Bayly, 1999):

India then is not and never has been a monolithic 'caste society'. It may even be that one day the principles and usages of *jati* and *varna* will lose much or all of their meaning for Indians living both within and beyond the subcontinent. Nevertheless, if one is to do justice to India's complex history, and to its contemporary culture and politics, caste must be neither disregarded nor downplayed—its power has simply been too compelling and enduring.

For some twenty years now, we have been witnessing a two-fold movement of Westernization and Sanskritization of behaviour patterns and values. On the one hand, the new post-Independence middle class, numbering 100 to 200 million people, have abandoned the austerity and reserve of their parents and taken to consumerism (Varma, 1998). On the other, it is this very middle class, better educated and trained in the modern professions, which shows a penchant for reviving the rituals and classical values still greatly revered by the traditional cultured milieu. It may well be that once Nehru's secular era is left behind, reformist, nationalist and neo-Hindu movements would perpetuate the nineteenth-century discourses of their predecessors by merely modernizing them. The essential current has remained nationalist, and the political formations that represent it are now in power.

II. The Politics of Business History and Strategies of Five Industrial Empires

ANNE VAUGIER-CHATTERJEE

Within the framework of an economic policy based on the three principles of self-sufficiency, protectionism, and primacy of the public sector, India presented a fertile ground for the growth of vast family-owned industrial empires that cornered the lion's share of the domestic market. Tata, Birla, Godrej, Bajaj, Ambani are those titans of industry omnipresent in the economic and social environment of India, whose history and strategies mirrored the overall evolution of the economy. These great names do not, however, form a homogeneous whole on the sociological front. This is illustrated in the first part of this second chapter, through the brief personal itineraries profiled below in terms of their place in the genealogy (first, second, third generation), the business community to which they belong (Parsi, Marwari, Gujarati, etc.) and also their educational and professional backgrounds (see pp. 66–76). The report then analyses the creation and evolution of these industrial empires, as well as their degree of involvement in the political and economic life of the country from a historical perspective, that is from the beginning of the twentieth century to 2000. Indeed, during the 1930s and 1940s, these great entrepreneurs played a considerable role in the struggle for independence. It is important to assess and further define this role by examining the nature of their relationship with the leaders of the national movement such as Jawaharlal Nehru and Mahatma Gandhi (see pp. 76–80). Then, after Independence in 1947, and during close to four decades, these businessmen remained under Congress dominance, adapting themselves willingly or unwillingly to the successive leaders who came to power (Jawaharlal Nehru, his daughter Indira Gandhi, her son Rajiv Gandhi, and lastly

Narasimha Rao). During this period of so-called Congress hegemony (1952–89), except for the brief Janata government interlude of 1977–80, the rapprochement or aloofness of businessmen *vis-à-vis* political leaders occurred in phases, depending upon the acceptance or non-acceptance of economic policies and rules imposed by the government. This necessarily impacted on the evolution of the Indian industrial landscape (see pp. 81–92). Lastly, in the early 1990s, the political landscape underwent radical change, subsequent to the decline of the Congress party and the emergence of new political formations on the national scene. It was also the era of the great financial crisis of 1991 and the reforms that followed, namely the abandoning of the mixed economy model in favour of liberalization of the markets. In this chaotic scenario, the fourth and last chapter of this study attempts to assess the capacity to adapt, or on the contrary, of resistance of these great industrial families, the new rules that governed their decisions, the stand taken by them *vis-à-vis* the political leaders in the context of an extremely volatile political environment—for not less than six governments came to power in ten years (see pp. 92–100).

ORIGINS, ESTABLISHMENT AND DEVELOPMENT STRATEGIES

Two Old Marwari Families: Bajaj and Birla

Bajaj and Birla are two well-established Marwari families with similar trajectories. The solidity of their links and family networks, but above all the evolution of their respective business activities have enabled them, in the space of a century, to make a successful transition from a traditional and very orthodox lifestyle to a modern one, with inputs from abroad. Their rise within a span of three generations followed the economic evolution of the country.

Bajaj, Generation I   Jamnalal Bajaj (1889–1942), the founder of the group, was adopted in 1894 by the Marwari merchant Seth Bachraj Bajaj. Today the group is a conglomerate of Rs. 60 billion, whose business activities range from two-wheelers to sugar, including electrical goods, the iron and steel industry, etc. In 1907, at the age of 18, Jamnalal Bajaj inherited his adopted father's worldly goods and took charge of the family enterprises, in particular the cotton industry, in which he met with great success. In 1913, he moved to Bombay, where through his connections with other industrialists, like David Sassoon, his business prospered. At the time, entrepreneurs followed a strategy of mutual collaboration rather than competition. Hence he started the New India Insurance Company Ltd. with the Tatas, that he managed until 1925. In 1926 his company was registered. He then launched Bachraj & Co. Ltd. in association with other Bombay business houses. He was also responsible for setting up Hindustan Iron and Steel Products, which later merged with Mukand Iron and Steel Works and Hindustan Housing Company.

Jamnalal Bajaj's son Kamalnayan Bajaj (1915–72) succeeded him in the early 1930s and also contributed to the consolidation of the paternal empire. Brought up according to his father's Gandhian ideas in the Spartan atmosphere and ascetic discipline of the Wardha (Gujarat) *ashram*, he too played an active role in politics. He first represented the Congress in Parliament, then later the Congress(O), the breakaway faction after its historic split in 1969.

Bajaj, Generation II

Kamalnayan's son, Rahul Bajaj, born in 1938, took over the reins of the empire in 1964. He started his career as deputy director of Bajaj Tempo Ltd. at Akurdi near Pune (Maharashtra). In 1970, he became executive director of Bajaj Auto Ltd., then chairman of the company in 1972. A third-generation Bajaj, his rise was phenomenal. He initiated a new style, combining tradition and modernity. He was a product of two worlds, the local Indian reality combined with an openness of mind associated with an excellent education. After a brilliant performance at the Cathedral and John Connon School in Bombay, he studied economics at St. Stephen's College in Delhi, and obtained his B.A. degree in 1958. Four years of practical training in the Bajaj companies completed the theoretical education. After he went to Harvard, where he took an MBA in 1964. Although Rahul Bajaj, who today presides over the Confederation of Indian Industry (CII), may not have his predecessors' political ambitions, he nevertheless moves within the circles of

Bajaj, Generation III

power. He maintained close ties with the undivided Congress. Unofficial adviser to Rajiv Gandhi, he was also a member of Sharad Pawar's (four times Chief Minister of Maharashtra) kitchen cabinet. Nevertheless, Rahul Bajaj prefers to keep a low profile. Contrary to many industrialists of his generation, since 1965 he has made his home within the family's industrial complex at Akurdi (near Pune, Maharashtra). Through this, he wishes to project the image of a man close to the middle classes. This is reflected in his style of dressing and his relationship with his staff.

Bajaj, Generation IV

Rahul Bajaj's succession is ensured by his two sons. Rajiv, the elder, born in 1966, has been responsible for marketing and product development since 1994. His second son, Sanjiv, born in 1969, has also accepted his share of the responsibility. Thus, since 1926 the Bajaj family, archetype of the joint family (see pp. 24–9), has not undergone any divisions. This has served to strengthen the emblematic character of this Marwari clan, whose name is now associated with the scooters that it sells all over the world.

Birla, Generation I

Another jewel in the Marwari crown is the Birla group, whose branches spread from Calcutta to the various states of the federation, and also outside India. Its interests are widespread, ranging from cement to synthetic textiles, palm oil, etc. The genesis of the Birla empire, like that of the Bajaj, goes back to the beginning of the twentieth century. Its founder, Ghanshyam Das Birla (1894–1983), came from the Shekhawati region of Rajasthan. Like many Marwaris, he chose Bengal (Calcutta) as the headquarters of his commercial activities. It was a natural choice as Calcutta, along with Bombay, was one of the principal business centres of the country. Towards 1910, when he was 16 years old, he and his brother Rameshwardas (R.D. Birla) ventured into the jute trade. His start-up capital of Rs. 2 million in 1914, quadrupled by 1918. The brothers set up the first Indian jute mill in 1919, then diversified into cotton, opening two cotton weaving-mills in Delhi and Gwalior. The head-quarters of the company, however, remained in Calcutta. On the eve of World War II, the firm Birla Brothers ranked thirteenth among Indian firms, with assets totaling Rs. 48.5 million. Very quickly G.D. Birla gained a certain prestige among the Marwari associations. He was one of the rare persons of his generation to master English and understand the workings of the Western mind. This made him the natural spokesman of his community. When, at the turn of the century, he tried to break the rigid Marwari code of behaviour, he incurred the ire of the more orthodox members of his community. Later, when the same pioneering spirit induced him to break away from the traditionally narrow sphere of operations to which Indian businessmen limited themselves, he encountered resistance from the British, who saw it as an invasion of their preserve.

The youngest of his three children, and his favourite, showed the same spirit of enterprise early in life. Basant Kumar (B.K. Birla) launched out on his own in 1945, by entering the tea industry, which at that time was entirely controlled by the British. It was an activity that his father associated with the *zamindars*, the landed aristocracy. Along with tea, he continued with the more traditional activities of the group, which he entered in 1951, by joining Century Mills. *Birla, Generation II*

Next, it was the turn of Basant Kumar's only son, Aditya Vikram Birla (1943–95) to contribute to the development of the family empire by bringing his expertise to state-of-the-art sectors such as chemical engineering. Aditya Birla grew up in Calcutta and received his early schooling at an establishment created by his father. After this, he transferred to another local school, the Hindi High School. After passing his high school exam., he went to St. Xavier's College in Bombay, where he received his B.A. degree. In 1962, at the age of 19, Aditya became the first Birla to go abroad for higher studies. He returned from Boston with a degree from the Massachusetts Institute of Technology. The setting up of a textile mill, Eastern Spinning, marked his entry into the world of industry. In 1966, he acquired Indian Rayon, and three years later founded the first of his overseas projects, in Thailand. After buying Indian Rayon, Aditya Birla moved his headquarters to Bombay. He then continued with the expansion and diversification of his group. Within thirty years he had become the biggest producer of viscose in the world and had promoted two big companies, Indo-Gulf Fertilisers and Mangalore Refineries and Petrochemicals. He set up some seventy factories manufacturing acrylic fibre and *Birla, Generation III* aluminium. Under him the group became the leader in several sectors such as cement, palm oil, and chemicals.

Birla,
Generation
IV

The year 1983 marked a turning point in the history of the Aditya Birla group, as he inherited two of the mainstays of his grandfather's group, Gwalior Rayon and Hindalco. In the beginning of the 1990s, he planned fresh projects in new high-potential sectors: electricity, telecommunications and financial services. When he died in 1995, the Aditya Birla group's turnover amounted to Rs. 150 billion. His son, Kumar Mangalam Birla, born in 1967, manages the family business today. But conversely to the Bajajs, the ideal of an undivided family, the business was beset for more than a decade by family feuds over G.D. Birla's legacy.

Two Parsi Industrial Empires: Godrej and Tata

Godrej,
Generation
I

Like many Parsis, it was in Bombay that the former advocate, Ardeshir Burjoji Godrej, born in Zanzibar in 1868, founded his business in 1897. He started off by making locks and safes, and later diversified into toiletries and cosmetics. 'Self-reliance', 'swadeshi', and 'swaraj' set the guidelines for the house of Godrej. Ardeshir's brother, Pirojsha B. Godrej, born in 1882, took over the reins of the business in 1936 and consolidated the reputation for quality and durability of its products. Having mastered the new technologies (in particular the technique of steel lamination), he went on to make office furniture. After which he decided to diversify and specialize in the manufacture of medical equipment (examination tables and surgical equipment), which were in great demand during this period. It was through Pirojsha that the dynasty would be continued.

Godrej,
Generation
II

Pirojsha B. Godrej's three sons, Sohrab (born 1912), Burjor (born 1915) and Naoro (born 1916) have taken up the challenge. The elder Sohrabji (S.P. Godrej), after getting a B.Sc. from St. Xavier's College, Bombay, successfully developed the group's marketing and commercial divisions. Towards this end he integrated the commercial branches of the group. In 1973, he became chairman of Godrej Boyce and Godrej Soaps. His brother Burjor P. Godrej, after studying engineering and obtaining his doctorate in Berlin in the early 1930s, took over the management of the Lalbaug soap factory. The third brother, Naoro (Nava), was responsible for diversification of the group's manufacturing activities, and was responsible for bringing out the first locally-produced typewriter in 1953, as well as refrigerators.

Like the Birla and Bajaj families, the dynasty continued to grow. Burjor's two sons, Adi, born in 1942 and Nadir, born in 1951, represent the third generation. Both studied at the best American institutions. After doing his B.Sc. in engineering and M.Sc. in business management at MIT, Adi became director of Godrej Soaps and distinguished himself with his considerable marketing talents. His brother Nadir, after a B.Sc. in chemical engineering from MIT, an M.Sc. from Stanford and an MBA from the Harvard Business School, manages a state-of-the-art sector, Gujarat Godrej Innovative Chemicals. Naoro's son, Jamshyd, is executive director of Godrej and Boyce Steel Business. Unlike other prominent industrial families (such as Birla), the Godrej family has not undergone any divisions. *Godrej, Generation III*

The Parsi family, Tata, is descended from a line of Zoroastrian priests (*dastur*), a hereditary charge that Nusserwanji Tata was the first to abandon in 1840. At this time, he changed his profession to become a banker in Bombay, and started trading with China. Thereafter, he opened branches in Hong Kong and Shanghai. On his return to India, he founded the Tata business house in Bombay. *Tata, Generation I*

His son, Jamset Nusserwan Tata (1839–1904) was a no less legendary and successful figure. He rallied Indian industrialists to the cause of national development, while not rejecting the indispensable technical inputs of his Western partners, in order to modernize the industrial and services sectors. He launched his first industrial venture, an oil extraction unit, Alexandra Mills, in 1869. He was among the first to explore the possibilities of the cotton industry, and for this did not hesitate to open new mills near the cotton-producing centres. Thus in 1894 he created a spinning and weaving factory, the Empress Mills at Nagpur (Maharashtra). In 1886, he set up a spinning unit at Bombay, and a second one at Ahmedabad (Gujarat). His *Tata, Generation II* originality and spirit of enterprise gave India her first luxury hotel, the Taj Mahal Hotel, in Bombay, whose foundation stone was laid in 1898.

Tata, Generation III

Struggling against an unco-operative government, but also technical handicaps and financial constraints, J.N. Tata died before his last dream, the creation of a steel-manufacturing mill, could be realized. It was to be fulfilled by his children and their cousin Ratan D. Tata (1856–1926), who was adopted and taken into Tata Sons in Bombay around 1870, after having spent his early years in a small Gujarati town (Navsari). The Tata Iron and Steel Company (TISCO) was created in 1907. It started producing steel as early as 1911. The Tata Hydroelectric Power Supply Company commenced supplying Bombay with electricity in 1915. The Tata enterprises proved that Indian industrialists could make their dreams come true before the transfer of power. It rapidly became one of the most important non-European business houses and carved a solid reputation for itself by its commitment to development, particularly in the sectors of science, technology and education (Harris, 1958).

Tata, Generation IV

A new stage was reached with Jehangir Ratan Dadabhoy Tata (1904–93), one of R.D. Tata's three sons. A product of two cultures, born in France of a French mother and Parsi father, J.R.D. Tata spent his childhood between France and Japan and only settled in India in 1925 at the age of twenty-one. Passionate about flying and planes, he launched Tata Airlines in 1932. He became chairman of the group that, in 1938, became the biggest in India. In 1945, he created, in collaboration with Daimler Benz, the Tata Engineering and Locomotive Company (TELCO), a major manufacturer of commercial vehicles (buses and trucks). The two principal production centres of the Tata group were Jamshedpur (TISCO) and Mithapur (Tata Chemicals). The business house of Tata was Westernized both in its habits as well as in its managerial culture. For example, the group was the only one to recruit retired senior civil servants (former members of the Indian Civil Service), thus maintaining a direct link with the colonial state. In consequence, rival groups accused Tata of a preferential policy *vis-à-vis* Europeans.

The vital question of succession came up repeatedly within the group. The genealogy of the Tata family is undoubtedly more complex than that of Birla or Godrej for it is constituted not of descendents in the direct line, but distant relatives. Thus as J.R.D. did not have a son, the contendors for the throne were many. One of them, Ratan Tata, born in 1937, a distant relative of J.R.D. (see Appendix 3), emerged from the shadows in 1981, when he became chairman of Tata Industries (J.R.D. was then 78 years old). After having obtained a degree in architecture and civil engineering from Cornell University in 1962, he left the United States for India, where he worked for six years in TELCO, Jamshedpur. Since then his standing in the group continued to improve. The 1980s were marked by intense speculation over the question of succession: it was a choice between Ratan and the old guard formed by Nani Palkhiwala, Darbari Seth and Russi Mody. But Ratan Tata had the entrepreneurial profile of his generation. In 1991, he succeeded J.R.D. as Chairman of Tata Sons. He was given preference over Russi Mody, then chairman of TISCO. In 1993, Ratan Tata took over even this chairmanship, after a highly publicized battle. A year later, in 1994, Darbari Seth resigned as chairman of Tata Chemicals and Tata Tea. Gradually, the old guard and directors of the group were replaced, and Ratan Tata's 'vision' was confirmed. The sale of TISCO's cement division to Lafarge, the launching of the car Indica, the restructuring of TELCO, the appointment of new top executives, the Tata code of conduct and a new logo, were its expressions. The aim of a more unified group, however, sharpened the conflicts, a result as much of resistance from within the enterprise, as of the government's liberalization policy of the early 1990s. This led to a recession in several sectors of the group's activities, namely steel, automobiles and chemical products (*Business World*, 13 September 1999: 16–25).

Tata, Generation V

The Young Ambani Group

The Ambani group has a unique place among India's prominent industrial families. Whereas Tata and Birla can boast of more than a century of history, the Ambani business goes back approximately forty years. But, like the pioneers of Indian

Ambani, Generation I

industry of the late nineteenth century, Dhirubai Ambani, its founder, did not shy away from hurdles in the establishment of his empire. Born in 1932, in Gujarat, the son of a teacher of modest means, he gave up the idea of higher studies and, following in his elder brother's footsteps, went off to Aden to seek his fortune and support his family back home. His path was that of a self-made man. His initial training was in Burmah Shell, a British petroleum company, where he started as a pump attendant and later became a salesman. After that he was employed in A. Beese & Co., an affiliate of Burmah Shell. With this experience behind him, he came to Bombay in the late 1950s and founded, after borrowing Rs. 15,000, a trading house, Reliance Commercial Corporation. Initially, Reliance Commercial Corporation was basically an export house, exporting mainly spices to the Gulf countries (ginger, cardamom, and cashew nuts), but also other goods such as sugar, clarified butter and sand. D. Ambani fulfilled specific export orders from the Gulf countries and this flexibility and a capacity to take risks explain the success of his business. In the mid-1960s, the government introduced measures to boost exports. It allowed profits realized through the export of rayon to be used for importing nylon. D. Ambani therefore changed his line of business, moving from spices to textiles directly and immediately. In 1966, he purchased a textile factory at Naroda near Ahmedabad. This was the start of an upward spiral. At the same time he began to diversify and thus gradually laid the foundations of an empire which ranged from activities as diverse as petrol refineries to synthetic textiles—a model of vertical integration. The group's profits also increased after the government, in 1971, authorized the import of polyester fibre against nylon exports. Reliance Commercial Corporation fulfilled 60 per cent of the exports generated by the government's new step. It remained its principal beneficiary until 1978, when the rule was revoked. Ambani then turned to the Russian and Polish markets, and also exported massively to Zambia, Uganda and Saudi Arabia. If D. Ambani proved different from other entrepreneurs because of his capacity to take risks and his anticipation of market trends, he was also the first industrialist to construct factories of international stature, in terms of both quantity and quality of the goods produced. The purchase of ultramodern equipment at the cutting edge of technology is another explanation for his business success. In 1975, a World Bank team which had come to inspect twenty-four textile mills in India, observed that only Reliance met the criteria of excellence in conformity with international standards. In 1978, Ambani also explored the domestic market. He managed to make a breakthrough thanks to a spectacular publicity blitz at the launch of his brand—Vimal. He got around the distribution network by opening his own shops: one per day between 1977 and 1980, or 20,000 by 1980, covering the entire territory with 1,000 franchised outlets. But like other Indian entrepreneurs, expansion was restricted by the stifling governmental controls. So be it. He also made a breakthrough on the capital markets and gained the confidence of small investors.

Despite the originality of its methods, the Ambani group, at the social level, reproduced the model of the family-run enterprises of the nineteenth century. Dhirubai's two sons, Mukesh (born 1957) and Anil (born 1959), educated respectively at Stanford and Wharton, took over the family business in 1986. As vice-presidents of Reliance, they are the decision makers of the group in their capacity as heirs of the emerging dynasty, but also as capable entrepreneurs with prestigious educational degrees. But far from being rigid, the managerial structure of the group is extremely flexible, both in its recruitment strategy, as well as in the running of the business. The senior management is primarily composed of a combination of Dhirubai's former associates, the financial intermediaries of his first projects, who since 1994 have acted as consultants to the group. Then there are managers with a particular expertise, mostly former public-sector officials. The Ambani group is one of the few businesses to tap this particular resource. Lastly, and more recently, it is also composed of young executives, educated in the best Indian and American business or technical schools (Piramal, 1996: 80). As in the other big industrial families which had preceded it, the second generation of Ambanis is also keen to take up social and philanthropic work. The chairmanship of the Dhirubai Ambani Foundation Trust is held by Mukesh's wife, Nita Ambani. Following the examples set by Godrej and Tata, the Trust has undertaken the construction of a township

Ambani, Generation II

for its workers, with lodging, schools and health facilities for the approximately 3,000 employees of the Jamnagar refinery. More recently, the Trust has also opened schools near the Hazira and Patalganga factories, as well as a hospital near Bombay (*India Today*, 26 April 1999).

DURING BRITISH INDIA (BEFORE 1947)

DIVERGENT APPROACHES TO POLITICS

Gandhi and Business Class

During the struggle for Independence, which coincided with the period between the two world wars, Indian businessmen assumed an ambivalent relationship with the political class, in particular with the Congress party (founded in 1885), spearhead of the nationalist movement. At Bombay, the commercial pulse of the country in the early 1920s, the entrepreneurs, in majority Parsis, deliberately held themselves aloof from politics. Engrossed in their business affairs, these first and second generation immigrants to Bombay were close to the British. It was in their interest to maintain the status quo. But Gandhi's arrival on the political scene drastically transformed this relationship. The Marwari and Gujarati merchant communities immediately manifested support for the Gandhian principles of *swadeshi* (encouraging people to buy Indian goods) and *swaraj* (political independence) (Markovits, 1985). But the business class's involvement in the freedom struggle led by Gandhi had its own rationale. Thus, the Bombay businessmen almost unanimously joined the fight against the British 'black laws' (the Rowlatt Bill of 1919) authorizing internment without an arrest warrant and court cases *in camera*, violation of private property, and individual security. On the other hand, they were against Gandhi's new weapon—*hartal* (closure of shops and markets), which was economically harmful to them. Thus, when Gandhi launched his first civil disobedience campaign of passive resistance in 1921, the industrialists reacted by signing a petition against such practices. They immediately formed a committee against the non-cooperation movement, secretly financed by R.D. Tata in the name of another Bombay businessman, Purushottam Thakurdas (Tripathi, 1991: 165). On the whole, rare were the great families, with the notable exception of the patriarch of the house of Godrej (Ardeshir Godrej), who financed the non-cooperation movement by contributing to the special fund created for this purpose, the Tilak Swaraj Fund. It is only in the early 1930s that Indian businessmen really began to show a solidarity that led to the development of a logic of economic action (see pp. 78–80 below).

The trajectory of two Marwari industrialists, Ghanshyam Das Birla and Jamnalal Bajaj, is a good example of an attitudinal difference *vis-à-vis* the Mahatma, and generally speaking, the dilemma faced by businessmen during the two decades of political turbulence (1920–40) that preceded Independence. Jamnalal Bajaj entered the political arena in 1920, encouraged by Mahatma Gandhi. An unconditional ally of the Mahatma's, he contributed substantially to the Congress coffers, whose de facto treasurer he became, as well as to the Mahatma's social projects. A member of the party's Working Committee, he accepted the consequences of his political choice and was imprisoned five times between 1923 and 1940 (Nanda, quoted in Tripathi, 1991: 191).

Bajaj and Gandhi

On the other hand, Ghanshyam Das Birla's relationship with Gandhi and the Congress party was more complex. Birla's chief difficulty lay in the fact that he wished to alienate neither the Congress nor the British government. Birla was in fact a fledgling entrepreneur when the Bengal Governor appointed him to the Legislative Council of the province, so that he could calm the nationalist fervour of the young Marwaris. Later, the political ups and downs and the ideological controversies never caused him to deviate from his business activities. At the end of the 1920s, he joined the Central Legislative Assembly as the representative of Lala Lajpat Rai and Pandit Malvaiya's nationalist party. During this phase of political transition, he remained a favourite of the British government. Despite his sporadic support of the Mahatma, he remained very circumspect and carefully distanced himself from the Salt March of 1930. Yet, despite this ambivalent attitude to nationalist politics, Birla very early accepted the task of defending the interests of Indian business and industry, playing a pioneering role in this respect. He was one of the few Indian industrialists to participate in the Round Table Conferences of 1931 and

Birla and Gandhi

1932, historic negotiations between the Indians and the British.

The Tata group also played a discreet role in the Independence struggle. Although J.N. Tata had been one of the spearheads of the nationalist movement under the leadership of his sons Dorab and Ratan, the group later stopped all political activity. Several of Tata's directors also joined the ranks of those opposing the non-cooperation movement, a result of the closer ties that developed between Tata and the British during World War I. The British government was the principal buyer of Tata products and Tata was the sole supplier of steel and rails to the railways and the national arsenals. The tension between major Bombay industrialists and the Congress party reached its height during Nehru's visit to that city in 1936. Worried by the 'socialist' tone of his presidential speech at Lucknow in 1936, twenty-one Bombay traders—all associated with the Tata group—signed a petition against the direction that Nehru's economic policy was taking (*The Times of India*, 20 May 1936). G.D. Birla, as mediator, immediately tried to mend the breach, but it was only after several years that a rapprochement between Tata and Nehru could be effected. In 1939, faced with a strike in their Jamshedpur factory, Tata agreed to mediation by Nehru (Tripathi, 1991: 174).

COMMON ECONOMIC STRATEGY

Estimating that the balance had weighed too long in favour of the British firms in India, who had formed their own chamber of commerce, the Associated Chambers of Commerce (ASSOCHAM), G.D. Birla took the initiative of creating, in 1927, a rival organization: the Federation of Indian Chambers of Commerce and Industry (FICCI). Although FICCI was not representative of all the Indian business communities, it rapidly became, unlike the ASSOCHAM of the epoch, an important forum for the expression of Indian views on economic policies. However, despite the desire to give this new organization a pan-Indian character, it continued to mirror the unending family, caste and regional conflicts which divided the business community. Apart from a few Parsis, Muslims, Bengalis and

Chettiars, FICCI was in the beginning largely dominated by the Calcutta Marwaris and the Bombay Gujaratis. But the Marwari community was itself very fragmented. At this time a breach developed, which would continue to widen, between a group with nationalist ideals and reformist aspirations, represented mainly by G.D. Birla, and a more orthodox, conservative group, ideologically closer to the colonial power. This rival group to Birla kept its distance from the Federation for close on ten years. South Indian businessmen (the Chettiars of Tamil Nadu, for example), although they were represented in FICCI, were also relatively indifferent to it. Lastly, the Bombay textile manufacturers association (Bombay Mills Association), the most important association of industries under Indian control, refused to join the ranks of such an organization. In particular, it was wary of the presence, at the head of the federation, of fiery nationalists such as G.D. Birla who showed his pro-Congress sympathies too openly for their comfort. Also, at its inception, the FICCI committee had the great disadvantage of not being able to count among its members most of the great names of Indian industry, especially the Tatas. The latter did not join the Federation, except for a brief period in the late 1930s. In 1939, the Tata representative left the Federation in the face of mounting tension between the Congress party and the British government, which was seen as damaging to the group. This setback somewhat destroyed the *raison d'être* of an organization intended to provide backup in Delhi for all Indian economic agents. The unbalanced composition of FICCI members is also explained by the greatly divergent interests and concerns of its members, in particular of the Calcutta business circles, represented by the Calcutta Chamber of Commerce, and of its counterpart in Bombay, the Indian Merchant Chamber, which represented mostly traders. This cleavage between the two economic poles of the times, Bombay and Calcutta, also found an echo in FICCI. Thus, despite its claim of being the economic arm of the Independence movement, the absence of a clear definition of its ideological choices, and competition from other chambers of commerce, rendered the relationship of FICCI with political leaders complex from the outset. Nevertheless, the creation of FICCI remains an important step in a process that would lead to a more harmonious mobilization of the

Indian business community, and which found expression in the Bombay Plan.

Even if unity in business forums was not always easy to attain, the representatives of the great industrial families did, however, share the same conception of economic policy. The choice of a strong state structuring and boosting economic development was unanimous in the 1940s. This trend was reflected in the National Planning Committee of 1938, presided over by J. Nehru. Similarly in the Bombay Plan of 1944, which was the work of a think tank of industrialists, in particular Tata and Birla (Birla, 1944). The Bombay or Tata–Birla Plan was an ambitious plan for economic reconstruction that, even before the end of World War II, sought to treble the national income and to double the per-capita income in fifteen years. Industrialization played a crucial role in this endeavour, accounting for 45 per cent of total investments. Priority would hence be given to the heavy industries, in order to promote development and reduce dependence on foreign countries. But it was also suggested that all sectors of economic activity be placed under the tight control of the state, temporarily alienating free enterprise, and that the redistribution of wealth be ensured by administered prices, a restriction on dividends, and the levying of taxes. State intervention was thus considered an essential dimension of national planning, and a guarantee of more effective income redistribution. This flexibility of businessmen with regard to the economic and political constraints that such choices require, can only be explained by the particular context of war. The authors of the Bombay Plan were in fact far from sharing the Nehruvian concept of planning. For them it was the state that was at the service of capitalism. In fact, they were at pains to distinguish an 'interim period' during which development would take place strictly within the framework of the Plan, and a second period characterized by economic revival, free from all these controls, once the minimum level of development had been attained. While leaving no room for doubt as to their choice of an economic system, they also recognized the possibility of the state exercising a permanent control on certain industries.

UNDER CONGRESS DOMINANCE (1947–91)

NEHRUVIAN SOCIALISM

Nehruvian socialism and the mixed-economy model which *Nehruvian* resulted from it, has caused much ink to flow. It took some *Socialism* years to establish itself after Independence and the Partition of 1947. In the aftermath of these events the new leaders had to define the role of the state in the national economy. The matter was of considerable importance for, in this period of transition and ideological groping, Nehru was attracted to the Soviet model with the state as entrepreneur. During its plenary session in November 1947, the All India Congress Committee (AICC) reiterated its preference for an economy guaranteeing maximum levels of production but without private monopolies or concentration of capital. This choice was re-affirmed by the economic reforms committee that, in its desire for social justice, wished to redistribute income and prevent excessive disparities in the process of industrialization to come. These rather radical choices came as a shock to the industrial families, already reeling under the anti-rich budget and the economic chaos resulting from the partition of the subcontinent. A compromise would be found in the Industrial Policy Resolution of 1948.

The Industrial Policy Resolution (IPR) of 1948 was in fact a *Industrial* compromise, which aimed as much to satisfy the diverse *Policy* interests of the Congress party and of a composite government, *Resolution* as of the rest of society, including private entrepreneurs. Its immediate objective was to re-launch production and instil confidence in businessmen by spelling out as quickly as possible the economic objectives of the government. To achieve this, it guaranteed that no nationalizat'on would take place before ten years (including the biggest industries), thus leaving a vast field for private enterprises to operate in, and made production and not redistribution, a priority. These concessions to the private sector were due to the influence wielded by right-wing political parties, such as the Jana Sangh (a forerunner of the Bharatiya Janata Party) and the Swatantra Party (see Appendix 4). The IPR established a tripartite division of powers, namely: (1) a state monopoly that included arms and ammunitions, railways and atomic energy; (2) exclusive right of the government to initiate new ventures in six sectors (coal, iron and steel, aeronautics, shipbuilding, telecommunications, mineral oils)—cooperation of the private sector in these fields was not excluded, but it was subject to government controls and regulations; (3) selective intervention by the state in all the other sectors left to private enterprise. Even if the Left was disappointed by what it felt was a betrayal of Nehru's socialist ideals, this declaration remained in reality the cornerstone of the mixed economy, although the terminology was never employed.

Planning I (First Five-Year Plan)   The ambiguity of the IPR of 1948, that affirmed the role of the state in the process of industrialization while acknowledging its dependence on the private sector, was also reflected in the formulation of the first five-year plans. Thus, the First Plan (1951–6) presented the public sector as a surrogate partner, providing a fillip to the private sector: (1) the emphasis was on production rather than redistribution; (2) the Plan was a modest one, it attempted to restructure and revive the economy which was bled white by the war; (3) priority was given to agriculture while industry was consigned to the backseat; (4) in the industrial field, developmental initiatives were left to the private sector.[1] In fact, the state's shortcomings called for cooperation and not competition between the sectors, which should 'function' like members of the same organization. There was however a 'head', which was the state: from 1951 onwards, the rationale of a planned economy applied to all levels of production. This meant ensuring the growth of industrial production and investments in conformity with the Plan, and also protecting and encouraging the small industries' sector. But despite the attraction that the Soviet model held for Nehru, he resisted the temptation of large-scale nationalization of the economy. In 1956, the government nationalized transport, electricity, insurance, but did not touch banks, steel, and coal. This 'restraint' certainly owed a lot to Mahatma Gandhi's influence on Nehru, and to his close ties with the major

[1] Indian Planning Commission, *First Five Year Plan*, New Delhi, 1953: 32–3.

industrial families (in particular Bajaj and Birla), to which was added the singular vision of private property as a 'trust'. Many Congressmen also adhered to this vision, rejecting Nehru's penchant for the socialist model. Thus the final choice of a mixed economy, justifying the anomaly of a private sector coexisting with a planned economy, becomes clear (Desai, 1999: 25).

A marked shift to the left occurred in 1955 with the Avadi Resolution of the Congress, which gave the public sector a greater role and imposed fresh constraints on the private sector (taxes on wages, nationalization of life insurance). These measures were followed by the Second Five-Year Plan (1956–60), which confirmed the socialist orientation of the economy. In keeping with this, the Industrial Policy Resolution of 1956 clearly defined the role of public and private capital by distinguishing three categories of activity: seventeen sectors in which all new initiatives were the prerogative of the state, twelve others where private investment was invited in collaboration with public capital, the others being left to private initiative. The IPR was favourably received in business circles insofar as it clearly demarcated the private sector's field of operations and temporarily removed the threat of nationalization (Kochanek, 1974). While some criticized it for its radicalism, the socialists felt that it was too moderate (Hanson, 1996).

Planning II (Second Five-Year Plan)

The Third Plan (1961–6) went one step further with the acceleration of industrial growth. Moreover, it redefined the role of the public sector, which was perceived as an alternative and a counter-weight to the concentration of economic power and monopolistic trusts in the hands of the private sector. This emphasis on the counter-weight role of the public sector was due to the expansion of the private sector beyond what was visualized. Thus the planners drew up a three-pronged strategy, which envisaged: (1) extension of the scope of the public sector; (2) tighter surveillance of the expansion of existing private businesses (namely by introducing licensing procedures prior to the creation of new industrial units); and (3) re-orientation of the economic policy with regard to the private sector in order to facilitate the entry of new entrepreneurs and break existing monopolies. All these steps, whose aim was to stop the

Planning III (Third Five-Year Plan)

formation of private monopolies and the concentration of economic power, ended by constituting what was described as the strictest and the most elaborate business legislation in the world (Hanson, 1966: 464–73).

In all, during the Nehruvian era, relations between the business world and the political world hinged around three distinct periods: (1) from 1947 to 1953, despite a rather critical existence in a volatile environment, the business world adapted to government policies, which were the reflection of a relatively ideological balance; (2) from 1954 to 1962, the private sector found itself in an ambivalent position *vis-à-vis* the economic line taken by the government, which oscillated between promises made in the 1940s and a stricter application of the Plan directives; (3) from 1963, the business barons opted for a markedly confrontational policy and resistance to government policies, which they considered harmful to their business interests. During this phase of Nehru's reign, J.R.D. Tata's relationship with Nehru was somewhat formal. The outward cordiality between the two men did not however hide their profound differences over the direction that the economic policy should take. For a long time Tata hoped to be able to soften Nehru's rigid ideas on socialism and thrash out matters close to his heart, i.e. nationalizations and the place of the public sector. The historian, A. Mukherjee, in his dialogues with Tata, noted the extreme frustration felt by one of the most dynamic entrepreneurs of his generation before Nehru's intransigence. The old industrial élite of Bombay, epitomized by Tata, better placed in the social hierarchy and better organized than the Marwari industrialists, was obviously in favour of economic liberalism. Established mostly in the Congress fiefs in Maharashtra and Gujarat, on the West coast where the Left had gained a foothold, it rebelled against the controls imposed by the Congress, which it considered a serious threat to private enterprise and high finance. This business élite reacted by creating first a Forum of Free Enterprise, then the Swatantra Party, the first political formation to fight the dominant economic consensus on the economic policy of the Congress (Kochanek, 1970). But it was a minor current for the majority of businessmen, in particular the Marwaris, preferred to use their powers of persuasion and their clout over the Congress, as well as their personal influence on Nehru. Jamnalal Bajaj was one such example. He had maintained close ties with Nehru, which were reflected in the friendship between the two families. G.D. Birla's attitude was the same. Despite his disillusionment, his loyalty to the Congress remained steadfast in keeping with his nationalist ideals (Birla, 1953: xv).

INDIRA GANDHI'S LICENCE RAJ

At Nehru's death in 1964, India went through a phase of tremendous political uncertainty. From 1962 to 1969, the Congress party was beset by severe internecine quarrels. The decline of its popularity resulted in its defeat in the 1967 elections in several states. However, despite this setback, the opposition parties did not succeed in forming stable coalition governments in their respective states (Rudolph et al., 1987). An era of turbulence followed, characterized by the defection of MPs from one party to another, a succession of cabinets, politicization of bureaucrats, but above all paralysis of the decision making process. And because of this political bankruptcy, the bureaucracy gained in importance and in independence. Increasing pressure was applied to accelerate the process of nationalization of the economy. From 1964 to 1969, the governments that succeeded Nehru set up four committees to reinforce their control over large-scale industries: the Mahalanobis Committee (1964), the Monopolies Inquiry Commission (1965), the R.K. Hazari Committee (1969), and the Industrial Licensing Policy or Dutt Committee (1969). From 1969, Indira Gandhi launched a radical programme of economic reforms including the nationalization of banks in 1969, of the insurance sector in 1971, of mines in 1973, of textiles in 1978—a programme that continued till the early 1980s. The Monopolies and Restrictive Trade Practices Act (MRTP) was promulgated in 1969. Any enterprise within the purview of the MRTP in relation to its assets or its market share now had to obtain government permission before going in for expansion or the creation of new enterprises.

National-izations

In concrete terms, during Indira Gandhi's two terms in office from 1966 to 1975 and 1977 to 1984, the Indian bureaucracy

Licence Raj

played a pivotal role in the management and realization of the five-year plans. It was the architect of a system of controls designed to regiment economic activity. Gradually, the administration fell into the habit of red tape, which effectively put a brake on industrial growth. All companies, even from the public sector, had to deal with administrative hurdles and procedural delays in their day-to-day working. Thus, if the Durgapur Steel Plant Ltd. wished to increase production, it had to apply to another government agency, Hindustan Steel Limited, which in turn addressed the matter to the Steel Authority of India. The project was examined by the Secretary of State for Steel, and then sent to the Planning Commission for approval, after which it was passed to the Economic Affairs Committee, and lastly to the Prime Minister's Office. The slowness of the procedures proved an obstacle to many a development project and increased out of all proportion the hold of bureaucrats over the political and economic life of the nation. This power was especially reflected in the personal links forged between the top echelons of bureaucracy and the heads of major industrial groups, an unavoidable result of the new power equations that had emerged. Some groups adapted to the new regulations, and isolated cases of economic growth could be seen, such as the Aditya Birla and Godrej groups. But generally speaking, the 1960s were lean years for the big industrial families. This fact is true for the economy as a whole—growth fell rather dramatically to 2 per cent per annum of GNP. India was left on the sidelines of global and regional economic development.

Tata under Indira

The business élite sometimes has a violent way of reacting, going so far as to question the validity of the Indian political system in terms similar to contemporary discourse. J.R.D. Tata, although close to the Congress, was deeply shocked by the nationalization of Air India and Air India International. In 1967, he reacted before the Ahmedabad Management Association in these terms:

Our Planners seem to forget that the flow of private capital into industrial investment requires an economic atmosphere and basic conditions which, through their economic policies, have largely disappeared. I need hardly mention the incredibly difficult, time-consuming and frustrating conditions under which Indian private enterprise, willing to undertake new projects or expand existing ones, has had to operate during the last few years. Had it been the Government's deliberate wish to discourage private investment in the industrial field, it could hardly have adopted a more appropriate set of economic and fiscal policies, measures and controls than it actually did. (Piramal, 1999: 496)

J.R.D. Tata remains incontestably one of the most ardent champions of private enterprise in respect of the reinforcement of government controls in the late 1960s. But his criticisms were not limited to business forums. In New Delhi, before the Planning Commission in August 1968, he declared:

As head of the largest industrial group in the private sector, I must be possessed of a tremendous concentration of economic power. As I wake up every morning, I carefully consider to what purpose I shall apply my great powers today. Shall I crush competitors, fire recalcitrant workers, topple a government or two? I wish Dr. Gadgil or another protagonist of this theory would enlighten me as to the nature of this great power concentrated in my hands. I have myself totally failed to identify it let alone exercise it. (Piramal, 1999: 497)

The same year, in a speech before the Indian Merchants Chamber, he denounced British bi-cameralism, which he felt was unsuited to the conditions, the temperament and the history of the country. Instead he proposed a presidential system in which the head of the government would be elected for a fixed period of time; he would be irremovable and free to govern through cabinets of experts. India would gain both in respect of political stability and expertise in the management of public affairs. This system would stop the country from slipping into communist totalitarianism, something that J.R.D. Tata and his allies greatly feared. In view of this, in his annual address at the Tata Iron and Steel Company, he declared:

These last twenty years, the liberty and the sphere of operations of the private sector has been subjected to a progressive but continuous erosion that has allowed the government to control production and distribution, which would have been inconceivable if these measures had been introduced in one go and is without precedence in non-totalitarian states. I do not deny that the intentions of our government are good but find it difficult to reconcile the public declarations on the economic policy of the Prime Minister, the ministers concerned and representatives of the government, with the manner and the pace at which our country is today being conducted on the path of totalitarianism. (Tata, 1971: 43)

Indira and Business Barons

The majority of the business élite agreed with J.R.D. Tata's critique. Some, decrying government inefficiency, went so far as to see military rule as the only solution (Kochanek, 1974). What clearly emerged from the seventy interviews with industrialists conducted by the American political scientist, Kochanek, in the late 1960s, was their concern over the quality (or its absence) of Indian leadership. They envisaged different political scenarios: some prophesied a process of political polarization around the Congress, others a swing to the right. In his blueprint, Kochanek aptly notes that the support for such a movement came from the newly-rich rural classes, and that the Jana Sangh (founded in 1951 and forerunner of the BJP) is the principal beneficiary because of its capacity to organize and mobilize the masses, particularly in the Hindi heartland states. The industrialists in favour of such a scenario were not particularly close to the party under discussion, but felt that it was the only right-wing party that had a chance of succeeding because of its appeal for the masses (Kochanek, 1974: 32–3). During this period, Indian business circles were in an awkward position *vis-à-vis* the ideological alignments dictated by expediency: should they pledge their allegiance to parties whose sympathies lay clearly with the private sector or should they conserve their influence within the ruling Congress?

Birla under Indira

The group most loyal to the Congress party, composed mostly of Marwaris, felt that despite its weaknesses the Congress was nevertheless the only option for business circles if they desired political stability—the Swatantra Party was politically too insignificant. G.D. Birla was its spokesman. Ten years older than J.R.D. Tata, it was easier for him to come to terms with the new regulations. As a result the Birla group prospered; in particular it set up Hindalco. In his speech on the eve of the 1967 elections, Birla warned businessmen against weakening the Congress in forthright terms:

I can tell you from my political experience there is not the slightest chance [for] any Swantantra Party or any Jana Sangh or any other party to come into power to replace the Congress. You can break the Congress. You can weaken it, but it is not going to help. You will be replacing this government by a Communist government and they will be the first to cut your throat. Do not make that mistake. Therefore, I tell you that there is no party in this country except the Congress which can give stability. (Kochanek, 1965: 8–9)

But there were many businessmen who, before the 1967 elections, disagreed with G.D. Birla's opinion on the importance of the Congress party. In fact his younger brother, B.M. Birla, went so far as to actively support opposition candidates, independents and dissidents. These businessmen thus hoped to reduce the majority that the party commanded in the Lok Sabha. And they succeeded, which greatly worried the Marwaris. They felt that the weakening of the Congress party would damage their business prospects, create a political vacuum instead of a stable government, and strengthen the leftist forces, especially the Communists and the trade unions. Despite all this, Birla became the largest Indian business house in 1976–7. The same year, an investigation by the *Economic Times*, a business daily, revealed that with assets worth Rs. 1,065 crores, Birla ranked first among the large groups, with Tata being relegated to second place with 975 crores. Although these figures should be treated with circumspection, they nevertheless indicate that the Tata group was the worst affected by Indira Gandhi's policies.

JANATA INTERLUDE

Tata and Janata

The Janata Party (see Appendix 5) came to power in 1979, not in response to an economic crisis but to a political one, and the popular condemnation of the Emergency imposed by Indira Gandhi from June 1975 to March 1977. The economic situation inherited by the government was comfortable. Paradoxically, it was a man who considered large-scale industry an 'abomination', the socialist and trade unionist, George Fernandes (Defence Minister in the Vajpayee government), who became Minister for Industry. He immediately condemned the great business houses for their 'collusive' attitude during the emergency. They were even subjected to a tirade at the annual meeting of the FICCI: 'How can men supposedly captains of industry and leaders in their domain kowtow to authority? What is this lack of strength of character which makes them behave like rats.' Moreover, on the question of nationalization, business circles were left in uncertainty in view of the contradictory declarations made by the new leaders. Although the Prime Minister, Morarji Desai, reiterated his belief in a mixed economy of the Nehruvian type and declared himself to be against nationalization, George Fernandes and Biju Patnaik, on the contrary, threatened to 'smash the Birla empire', 'to demolish the 20 biggest Indian industrial groups' and 'to nationalize Tata Iron and Steel Company'. On this last point, the suggestion aroused the indignation of the Jamshedpur workers and the project had to be abandoned. On the other hand, in 1977, Morarji Desai rescinded J.R.D. Tata's chairmanship of Air India—the price of the rapprochement of the latter with Indira Gandhi during the Emergency (1975–7). A tussle between the Janata leaders and J.R.D. Tata followed. J.R.D., worried by the critical situation the country was in, had in fact not been against imposition of the Emergency (Piramal, 1999: 510). In 1977, the Tata group had even donated Rs. 75 lakhs to the Congress-I (Piramal, 1999). After her re-election in 1980, Indira Gandhi showed her appreciation of Tata's stand by returning him to the board of management of Air India, without however restoring his status of chairman.

THE CHANGING 1980s

*Indira
Gandhi*

The return of Indira Gandhi to power in 1980 meant a break with the logic which had led to the policies initiated in 1969 and which continued during the Emergency. In economic terms, a change of direction was observed, marked by a hardening of the attitude towards the public sector, and compensated by a more favourable approach towards the private sector. In 1980, industrial policy was redefined, restoring the balance between the small- and large-scale industries. In the year 1982, a more pragmatic economic policy, free from dogmas, was conceived. It comprised two steps to boost investment: (1) an automatic expansion of the production capacity to the extent of one-third of existing production levels; (2) extension of the list of heavy industries, thus broadening the field of operations of the great industrial groups and firms regulated by the Foreign Exchange Regulation Act (FERA). The government also opened to the private sector certain industrial activities which had hitherto been the preserve of the state. This included electricity and oil refineries. Thus, Tata set up a 500 megawatt electric power station in Bombay. Similarly, the government decided to de-regulate the cement industry. Apart from this, it sought to boost investment by encouraging financial mobilization through the launching of public share issues. This policy was relatively successful since the capital mobilized by the private sector rose from 3 billion in 1980–1 to 5.29 in 1981–2 and 8.09 in 1983–4, an increase of 170 per cent in three years.

Economic policy was once more given a new direction by Rajiv Gandhi (1944–91). Nehru's grandson came to power in a landslide victory during the 1984 general elections, after his mother, Indira, was assassinated. Symbolizing a new generation, he broke away from the broad principles of Nehruvian policy. His experience abroad, his studies in England, his marriage to an Italian, motivated him to open the country to the outside world. He managed to get loans from the International Monetary Fund (IMF) to redress the country's economy and initiated the process of de-regulation and import liberalization. Although aware of the weaknesses inherent in the public sector, for political reasons he was not bold enough to undertake a radical reorganization of the public sector through massive privatization. But the enormous machinery of state control was revised, in particular the Monopolies and Restrictive Trade Practices Act, which represented an important means of slowing down development of large private groups. These measures were accompanied by fiscal reforms, encouraging enterprises to increase investment and production levels through a reduction in taxes and customs duties. The great originality of the Seventh Plan (1985–9) was that, for the first time, it gave the private sector an important role to play. The latter was asked to finance more than 50 per cent of the investments out of a total of Rs. 3,200 billion over a five-year period (Dorin, 1994: 158).

Rajiv Gandhi

Reliance

The best illustration of the fruits of this policy was the break-through made by the new Ambani group, Reliance Industries Limited (RIL), which very quickly distanced itself from the rest of the field. In an innovative move, Dhirubai Ambani chose to involve shareholders in his business ventures while most of the captains of industry played for time. The 1980s saw the emergence of a middle class, which was the best guarantee for the recruitment of shareholders, a cross-section of personalities from the private and public spheres with a certain political influence. Very rapidly Reliance took the lead in the private sector in terms of sales, profits, stock-market capital, and assets. The state had a stake in its capital but a minor one. The boss of Reliance had also made strategic investments in the political sphere, favouring the creation of an environment conducive to shareholder satisfaction. Ambani's 'accommodative' style of functioning between the world of business and the political class had a visionary quality. While Reliance proved that obstacles could be worked around to maximum advantage, there was a price to pay. In a recent study on the behaviour of family-owned businesses, Reliance figured at the bottom of the ladder in terms of ethics. This was damaging to its image (*India Focus*, Sept.–Oct. 1997).

FACE-TO-FACE WITH MARKET LIBERALIZATION (1991 ONWARDS)

DEALING WITH FOREIGN COMPETITION

Reforms of 1991

When V.P. Singh came to power in November 1989, he followed the line he had adopted as Rajiv Gandhi's Finance Minister. In 1990, a document entitled 'Towards a Restructuring of Industrial Commerce and Fiscal Policy', had been specifically proposed to reduce the degree of protection enjoyed by Indian industry, to gradually open the economy to foreign capital, and to devalue the rupee. These decisions gave rise to sharp reactions on the part of members of the Planning Commission, but thereafter events occurred in rapid succession. On May 1991 Rajiv Gandhi was assassinated in the midst of the election campaign and, in July, the country adopted a massive Structural Adjustment Programme (SAP) since India's external debt had risen to more than 70 billion, inflation touched 17 per cent and the exchequer had barely three weeks of foreign-exchange reserves left. It meant the bankruptcy of a system and the inevitable shift to a market economy, as the new government, led by P.V. Narasimha Rao, confirmed. A number of the new measures received a favourable response from the major industrial groups. Firstly, the 1969 anti-trust law was virtually abolished. Large businesses were henceforth allowed to exceed the limit imposed on expansion without prior approval. Secondly, the government did away with many of the stringent regulations of the Licence Raj: enterprises could now expand freely, apart from 18 sectors in which an administrative clearance was still the rule (coal, sugar, animal and vegetable oils, tobacco, automobiles, paper, space electronics, military equipment, certain chemical products and luxury goods). Thirdly, foreign investment in India was liberalized. According to an official announcement, all industrial activity had to be open to competition. The entry of foreign capital into India was not merely authorized because of a technological fallout or export benefits, but in order to expand the production capacity of the country. All investment to the extent of 51 per cent of the firm's capital was automatically accorded by the government in thirty-four priority sectors (in particular: metallurgy, electrical equipment, transport, industrial equipment, fertilizers, chemicals, agro-foods and tourism). At the same time, import of capital goods was liberalized. Various steps were taken to encourage exports. The public sector's sphere of operations was reduced. However, the latter retained arms and ammunition, atomic energy, railways, and diverse mining activities—but it lost steel, aviation, telecommunications and shipbuilding.

As a result of these measures, in September 1993, a group of industrialists from Delhi, Madras and Calcutta met in Bombay to discuss how best to tackle the problem of foreign competition, an inevitable corollary of the liberalization of 1991. Some kept their distance, such as Ambani, who declared: 'I am one hundred per cent in favour of liberalization, and I do not think there is one industrialist who is against it. But we have to protect our industry from all unfair competition.' Others, Aditya Birla for instance, acquiesced with the opinion of the members of the Bombay Club, without however joining it. According to

Bombay Club

an economist from the Tata group, Birla would have willingly joined the Club to help define fair rules of competition between Indian and foreign industries, but felt that the Club needed to change its reactionary image and reassure public opinion that members were not just interested in hiding behind the protectionist umbrella. Although the Club as a whole had adopted a defensive stance to deal with foreign competition, it is difficult to see what its members had in common. For Bajaj the stakes were obvious. As the government had prevented the industry from functioning independently for decades, it must now give Indian industry a chance to reorganize itself in order to compete with international giants. In the meantime, immediately after the open door policy was announced, several Indian companies sought foreign partners. Godrej for example entered into collaboration with Proctor & Gamble, and Tata entrusted Tata Oil Mills to a subsidiary of Unilever. But would multinationals mean the disappearance of Indian companies by the year 2000? This was a question that the corporate sector asked itself frequently in the face of these major upheavals. Two months after its first meeting, in November 1993, the Bombay Club presented a charter of demands in thirteen points to the Finance Minister, Manmohan Singh, and his adviser, Montek Singh Ahluwalia. The modes of financing and the necessity of lowering interest rates were emphasized. But according to experts, the Club was 'a group of inefficient producers fearing competition'. Many members deserted it then, fearing the bad press they would get before the leaders. By the end of 1994, Bajaj was the only member of the stillborn Club left (Piramal, 1997: 128). Accommodation and adaptation to the New Economic Policy (NEP) were the norm, and here too a compromise had to be made with the ruling élite, as the examples of Tata and Ambani well illustrate.

Ratan Tata, J.R.D.'s successor, had already envisaged new avenues to development in the 1980s. Taking note of the absence of any strategic guidelines, he had drawn up a new agenda called the 'Tata Strategic Plan'. According to him, after the phase of inertia generated by the Government's restrictive policies in the 1960s, it was imperative for the group to extricate itself from the production–sales logic and move into new areas of business activity. A second aspect was the financing of the group and the management of shareholders. Administered by a board of directors composed of non-family members, Tata Sons launched a rights issue in which all the companies of the group were involved (TISCO, TELCO, Tata Tea, Indian Hotels). From 1995 onwards, Tata companies continued to tap the capital markets. As for the group's relations with the government, particularly the Congress-led governments, two distinct scenarios before and after 1991 emerged. A shared sense of values and a common outlook between two contemporaries, Ratan Tata and Rajiv Gandhi, had contributed to a radical change in the group's attitude *vis-à-vis* the government. In recognition of this rapprochement, Ratan Tata was awarded chairmanship of Air India. He was also appointed special adviser to the Minister of Science and Technology. Still more significant, several projects outlined in the Strategic Plan of 1983, and rotting in dusty files in the Ministry of Industry, were now approved, especially the entry of the group into the petrochemicals sector, for which one of the directors, Darbari Seth, had been fighting for decades (Piramal, 1999: 399). But this happy phase ended with Rajiv Gandhi's term in office. Under the V.P. Singh Janata Dal government (1990–1) and the P.V. Narasimha Rao Congress government (1991–6), relations reverted more or less to their previous levels, as had the relations between Indira and J.R.D. This is illustrated by the difficulties the group had to face to launch the joint venture with Singapore Airlines, and the failure of its repeated attempts to have TISCO's mining rights in Orissa renewed.

In the Ambani case, just as the father was able to expand his empire under the Licence Raj, his two sons, Mukesh and Anil, have adapted to the orientation of the NEP. The Ambanis have been successful in their vertical integration programme, starting from textiles and polyester fibre and going up to petrochemicals. The latest strategic decisions of the group involve an activity situated at the top of the chain, namely the increase of its oil-refining capacity. Although traditionally close to the Congress, the Ambanis have taken care not to alienate the BJP (see Appendix 5). The only blemish in their record has been their financial backing of a BJP dissident, Shanker Singh Vaghela, in the 1995 and 1997 elections. After his election as Chief Minister of Gujarat, Vaghela, with astonishing speed, took the Hazira

Ambani and BJP

refinery project to its successful conclusion. In so doing, he is supposed to have incurred the displeasure of L.K. Advani, who is not seen as an ally of Reliance. In November 1998, the CBI ordered a raid on the group's headquarters in Bombay, on its Delhi offices, and also on the principal directors of the company (*Outlook*, 30 Nov. 1998). The Opposition perceived this raid as a BJP manoeuvre to promote its anti-corruption drive. Highly publicized, the pretext for this raid was the possession by Reliance of secret documents belonging to the Petroleum Ministry. It then becomes clear that the sum total of Reliance's influence over the Central government, irrespective of the leaders, has shrunk since the BJP-led coalition has been in power.

POLITICAL PATRONAGE AND ELECTION FUNDING

Funding of the Congress

From the early 1980s, the financial dependence of the Congress-I on the Indian business community has been diminishing. On the other hand, its financial links with foreign firms present in India, with which important contracts in the field of defence and infrastructure have been signed, have become stronger. The Congress-I leaders had ensured that fund-raising was centralized within the party, after which funds were dispatched to secret accounts abroad. During this period the Congress party did not tap regional and local-support networks to fund their election campaigns. After Rajiv Gandhi's election in 1984, efforts were initiated to put a stop to the 'briefcase policy', which was damaging the party's image. He lifted the ban on company donations to political parties, even as he took significant steps to relax controls, and initiated fiscal reforms to boost growth and reduce corruption. He restored the ceiling on donations to the extent of 5 per cent of the companies' net profits. By playing the transparency card with regard to political donations, Rajiv Gandhi managed to exploit the favourable climate created by international contracts finalized during his time in office. But midway during his tenure as Prime Minister, a number of scandals broke out (including the Bofors arms deal), compelling him to end the transparency experiment. By the early 1990s, the Congress had raised and spent more funds than all the other parties put together through a complex network of personal contacts and unwritten agreements.

The brief Janata interlude of 1989–91, and the return of the *Funding of Coalitions* Congress to power in 1991, goes to show that Indian businessmen of the 1990s, like those of the 1970s, preferred to finance political stability rather than ideologies. Narasimha Rao's Congress government (1991–6) continued the liberalization process, but like Rajiv Gandhi, he became implicated in a series of scandals, which are revealing of the unorthodox methods of political funding that are used. The failure of the Congress to win a majority in the 1996 elections and the 'United Front' coalition government experiment that followed, convinced everyone that political coalitions were here to stay. In 1998, the first BJP government in the national political history of India was formed. Ever since then, industrialists have put their money on the dominant political party in each state, whether regional or national. With the chronic political instability engendered by indecisive electoral verdicts and hung parliaments of the 1990s, industry is no longer in a position to finance political parties as generously as it had done in the past, especially if elections are frequently held (i.e. if they take place at intervals of less than five years). In 1993, the Confederation of Indian Industries (CII) set up a 'task force', which recommended that private contributions be tax deductible if the source of political funding is to be re-activated. But these propositions have had no impact, if we judge from the 1996 elections that marked a turning point in electoral fund raising. For the first time, many firms were not approached for financing the campaign (Sridharan, 1999: 240).

In a report submitted to the government in 1998, the Indrajit *Gupta Committee* Gupta Committee on electoral reforms proposed that political donations be maintained at 5 per cent of the net profits of firms of the three preceding financial years. These donations must be made with the approval of the company's shareholders, and not through a resolution passed by the board of directors, as the law had hitherto demanded. For greater transparency, the Gupta Committee thought it desirable that members of the board of directors declare their political choice—or even their affiliation to a party—during the general body meeting to decide on political contributions. Despite official recognition of private donations by Rajiv Gandhi in 1985, very few enterprises were ready to accept the conditions imposed by this transparency rule. Initially, these measures were supposed to highlight the role of the private sector in the democratic process. However, the prospect of discord during the annual general body meetings dissuaded most firms from following this line. Lastly, the threat of reprisals by the victorious party, to whose coffers an enterprise had not contributed, explains the hesitation on the part of firms to reveal details of their contributions. Nonetheless, a recent Supreme Court decree has directed political parties to identify and itemize donations in their accounts (it has also said that a candidate can exceed the ceiling on expenditure if his/her party agrees to bear the responsibility for the excess expenditure). This changes the modalities of funding of the big parties, especially the Congress and the BJP, that henceforth prefer to receive donations by cheque.

BJP and Business Class

The BJP was the first to implement this last reform by announcing that it would not accept donations exceeding Rs. 10,000 except by cheque. The donors falling within this category would all be mentioned in the party's newspaper, *BJP Today*. That no such list exists for donors exceeding this limit is probably not an accident. However, according to the Treasurer of the BJP, contributions by business groups constitute but a fraction of the party's funds. The major portion of BJP funds, as in the past, come from shopkeepers and small and medium entrepreneurs at the local and regional levels, as well as from supporters and party activists. Before it came to power in 1998, the party had not had much to do with big industrial groups. In the 1990s, however, several phases in the evolution of the relationship between prominent businessmen and the BJP can be distinguished. After a period of pessimism, businessmen recovered their confidence, which was accompanied by a rapprochement with the BJP. After its short stint in office of thirteen days in 1997, the party promised important concessions during its next term in office. Thus, on the eve of the 1998 general elections, a study on businessmen revealed that the majority of them were in favour of the BJP. This constituted a major change. For a long time, the BJP's exclusive and communitarian reputation, its marked preference for small- and medium-level traders, as well as its refusal to open the economy, had alienated the big groups. In its latest electoral programme, the BJP expressed its desire to continue the reform process by strengthening the *swadeshi* dimension in order to ensure the growth of the national economy, according to the principle: 'India will be built by Indians' (*Manifesto of the National Democratic Alliance*, 1999: 4). With this end in view, it proposed steps to boost national industry, so that it could compete with multinationals both locally and globally. In the face of 'the old leftist approach that wished industry to be controlled by the state, and the liberal approach that wishes market mechanisms to have free play, we reject both. The state and industrialists must work together to attain the key goals and encourage market dynamism through effective and regulatory mechanisms' (ibid.: 5).

The ruling BJP owes its present position to the support of twenty other political parties. Business circles are well aware of this and since the liberalization of the economy and the political instability of the last decade, have formed neutral Trusts in order to funnel money likely to be used for political purposes. On the eve of the 1998 general elections, the firm Tata Sons formed an electoral Trust to finance political parties. According to the rules of the Trust, half the funds were to be distributed during the election campaign, the other half after the poll results were announced in proportion to the respective weight of parties in Parliament. In reality, it is difficult to evaluate the disbursements made to parties. This Trust in fact has met with only moderate success and although open to outside firms, it is difficult to estimate how many companies, other than those from the Tata group, have contributed to the fund. Naturally, companies prefer a direct and one-to-one contact with parties, and feel that it is really for chambers of commerce such as CII or ASSOCHAM to fight for the collective rights of industry. Be this as it may, Grasim Industries Limited, spearhead of the Aditya Birla group, has also set up an electoral Trust based on this model. It only accepts donations from members of the group. What is important is the interest of the companies forming the Trust in each state. This logic is more economic than political. In view of its own financial interests, a company could finance a party in one state and its rival in another. One solution is for the big groups to come to an agreement to make the funding of parties public. One cannot, as a matter of fact, really correlate a

Electoral Trusts

reduction in election costs with a reduction in corruption and greater transparency of the government.

CONCLUSION

Today, nearly 80 per cent of Indian companies are still family-owned businesses. The five principal family groups presented here are heirs to Indian entrepreneurs who were able to prosper in a relatively stable political environment, in which the Congress party predominated for a long time. In order to arrive at this, they generally gave greater importance to their relationship with the government, than to their own development strategy. But in return, Indian capital benefited from protected markets within the framework of Nehruvian socialism, enabling these groups to expand disproportionately in the sectors reserved for them, and making them the substitutes for a faltering public sector.

Since the 1991 reforms, the facts of the case have changed. The overriding tendency is to diversify into areas that the government has now opened to the private sector, but which is harmful to the competitiveness of many a company. But as anywhere else, the rapidity of their response, their ability to adapt to change, their capacity to recruit talent, the acuity of their market studies, their level of innovation and enterprise, their business ethics and their general image will decide their future in the era of globalization.

Today the Tata group is in the process of restructuring itself and diversifying its business activity. Its major handicap is the uncertainty of its succession. The A.V. Birla group remains, by reason of its financial strength, one of the most reputable business houses, but its conservative mode of functioning acts like a brake in the exploration of new sectors. Bajaj, which also enjoys an excellent reputation, remains wary of joint ventures. The decision making process of the new Godrej management remains orthodox. The Ambani group, whose style is different, has lost some of its political clout today. In a changing economic universe, the only constant variable is the common desire of the titans of industry for political stability, a necessary but insufficient condition for the pursuit of reforms.

III. The Employer and his Enterprise
International Leather Shoemakers in Tamil Nadu

NICOLAS FLAMANT

The north of Tamil Nadu is one of the most important industrial centres of finished leather and shoes for the European, Australian and North American markets. Here as elsewhere, tanning in its traditional form has always existed, assigned to certain lower castes (SC)[1] that specialized in this work. But it was the Labbai Muslims who were responsible for its progressive industrialization during the nineteenth and twentieth centuries. The third chapter[2] of this book is based on *in situ* observations that show how and to what extent the culture of these Labbai entrepreneurs influences, indeed determines, the forms of management at different levels of the enterprise. It also shows how cultural and managerial backgrounds adapt to external logic and demands that bring about changes within the enterprise and its environment.

In order to grasp the rationale behind the development of the industry, and to provide the key to an understanding of management methods, the first section presents some cultural and religious reference points (see pp. 102–9).The second section shows how these factors intervene in the general organization of the industry, particularly with regard to management of capital, and the industrial strategies that are subjected to the rules imposed by the family and the community (see pp. 110–23).

[1] Scheduled Castes (Adminisatrive category which mostly gather those termed 'Untouchables' during the British time, and now 'Dalits'. See Chapter I for more details).

[2] This study was conducted under the 'Palar Valley' research project of the French Institute of Pondicherry (IFP).

The third and final section (see pp. 123–34) takes us inside the enterprise to observe its day-to-day management. Traditional cultural references also play an important role here, but they coexist with the new logic of social change introduced by industrialization and wages.

MUSLIM POPULATION AND MUSLIM ENTREPRENEURS

THE LABBAI COMMUNITY AND ISLAM

Islamization

The heterogeneity of the Muslim population in south India is due to the different processes of Islamization that have occurred in this region. Arab traders operating on the Kerala and Tamil Nadu coasts initiated one such process in the eighth century. One other process was started later in north India by Afghan and Mughal invasions of the twelfth and seventeenth century. Today, Muslims represent approximately 12 per cent of the total Indian population, but in Tamil Nadu this percentage is lower (about 9 per cent). However, the concentration is much higher in the northern part of the state. There are two historical reasons for this density. First, the town of Arcot was the administrative capital whose Nawab ruled the region until the mid-eighteenth century. Secondly, the development of the leather industry, in the course of the twentieth century, attracted other south Indian Muslims, in particular from the Tanjore and Erode regions.[3]

Labbai

The origin of the present-day Labbais is rather uncertain. British colonizers named the Tamil-speaking Muslims Labbai, to differentiate them from the Urdu-speaking Deccanis. It appears that the Labbais were generally low castes or those termed 'Untouchable' who had converted to Islam, even though some now affirm that they came from all the castes, including

---

[3] Today, this concentration is the cause of major tensions, particularly in agglomerations where the percentage of Hindus is higher. Such towns, closely monitored by the political and police authorities of the district, are zones where Hindu extremist organizations (Vishva Hindu Parishad, Rashtriya Swayamsevak Sangh and Bajrang Dal) as well as Islamic fundamentalist organizations (Tabligh-i Jamaat and Jamaat-i Islami) are active.

Brahmins. The Labbais reject the idea of caste stratification, which for them is a Hindu characteristic. However, the occupational specialization and endogamy (see pp. 19-24 above, pp. 110–11 below) of this community reveal its caste structure.

Whereas certain dominant Deccani *jatis* (see pp. 33–6) continued to pursue the intellectual professions (administration and teaching) that had ensured their dominance under the Mughals, the Labbais entered the fields of industry (especially leather and *beedi* manufacture) and trade (trading in hides as well as petty commerce as butchers, dealers in merchandise and groceries). These areas, which the Labbais now entered, had been left vacant by the Hindus during the Raj.

Professional Specialization

Matrimonial alliances between the Labbais and Deccanis are rare. The Deccanis are subdivided into different endogamous or restricted exogamous subgroups.[4] Endogamy is equally predominant in the Labbai community. Many families which specialize in an industry or trade, only marry into families in the same profession. In addition to this, economic criteria play a significant role in these alliances (Mines, 1972). Here the isogamic model prevailing in south India (see pp. 19–24) takes the form of alliances between families of equal social and financial status. In the industrial and urban milieu, this structure superimposes itself over class stratification. Tholpuram industrialists are a case in point. We notice that five or six prominent families who intermarry, control all the enterprises. The same is true of business executives—often distant cousins of the proprietors—whose close relatives (brothers, brothers-in-law) are generally of equal professional status.

Endogamy

GENESIS AND DEVELOPMENT OF THE
LEATHER INDUSTRY

The first tanning units were set up by Europeans in Madras at the beginning of the nineteenth century to supply Western markets (France, Great Britain and Netherlands) with skins. The

Tanneries (European)

[4] The Sayeds, who claim to be direct descendants of the Prophet Muhammad, the Sheikhs, the Pathans, the Khans, constitute the dominant *jatis*.

colonizers recruited Muslims, who did not have the same notions of purity and impurity as the Hindus,[5] to manage the units and the procurement of hides. But leather was handled strictly by certain lower castes. Very soon the region was not able to supply enough skins to satisfy the needs of European markets. It became necessary to look further afield and tap sources in north India. But transport delays and the rather hasty curing methods caused much of the stock to rot during transportation. Business became less and less profitable and working conditions very uncertain. In the mid-nineteenth century, the few European tanners in the area abandoned their factories.

Tanneries
(Muslim)

The Muslims then gradually gained a foothold in this sector. Some of them had been trained in management by the Europeans. Others started to create their own units. Along with the development of tanneries, they took over control of the trade networks within the British Empire. By the mid-nineteenth century, Muslims had the monopoly of both tanning and manufacturing, which they slowly mechanized. For approximately a century, that is till the end of the 1960s, these tanneries produced semi-finished leather according to the traditional vegetable-tanning methods.

Tanneries
(Modern)

From the 1950s, the government began to promote modernization of the leather industry. After Independence, leather ranked fourth in importance among Indian exports. It was sold as semi-finished leather to Great Britain, which enjoyed a quasi-monopoly on the product and its transactions. The quality requirement for intermediary tanning was not very strict. Leather pieces were simply graded and sold in lots. For the tanner, the relative advantage of this minor quality-requirement

---

[5] In Hinduism, leather is closely associated with the dismembering of carcasses, and therefore with death. Hence it carries the stigma of impurity and uncleanliness. Working with leather, from cutting up the carcase to tanning, is reserved for the lowest stratum in the hierarchy, the reverse of the ritual purity associated with Brahmins. In fact, working with leather and skins is one of the principal signs of 'untouchability' (Dumont, 1966).

was accompanied by the certainty of selling his product. But this situation strengthened the British position and subordinated production. Prices fluctuated widely and payments were always late. In the 1950s several delegations, consisting of entrepreneurs and representatives from the Ministry of Industry, went to Europe and America to meet foreign industrialists dealing in leather. In 1953, the importance of the leather industry to Tamil Nadu resulted in the setting up of the Central Leather Research Institute (CLRI) in Madras, for which Calcutta had also staked its claim. This organization played a substantial role in promoting research and introducing industrial innovations, in particular the chrome tanning method. This modern method increased productivity by reducing production cycles. It improved quality and helped to obtain a standard result despite materials of diverse quality. However, this new technology was incorporated very gradually. Most industrialists jibbed at making fresh investments and preferred to submit to the British monopoly, which despite its drawbacks, ensured the sale of their goods.

The Indian government encouraged industrialists to deal in finished leather, whose value-added for exports was greater than that of semi-finished leather. In 1972, the Seetharamiah Committee, composed of experts from CLRI and some pioneering industrialists, proposed a draft bill whose objective was to stop the export of skins and semi-finished leather through fiscal deterrents, and facilitate leather exports of finished products (garments, shoes, fine leather goods). The production of finished leather increased thereafter in India (see Figure 1) and broke the British monopoly. Several markets now opened for Indian tanners. Among the more important were the United States, and more so the USSR. During the 1960s, the tanneries became truly industrialized through large-scale adoption of the chrome method.

*Leather
Policy*

A second phase of industrialization now started immediately after the first drew to a close in the late 1970s. Some tannery owners set up factories to produce shoe uppers for European (Italians, Germans, Portuguese, Danes) but more importantly North American industrialists. During the 1980s, large industrial

*Shoe
Industry*

groups owned by a few Muslim families, the new local dynasties, were formed: several firms began to manufacture the complete shoe, and the shoe industry really took off (see Figure 1) and radically modified the socio-economic landscape of the towns of the region. A growing minority of high-caste Hindu entrepreneurs (Chettiars and Brahmins) now developed an interest in this sector. Their factories were mainly situated in the suburbs of Chennai (Madras). Besides these two communities, the towns also attracted industrialists from north India, as they offered many facilities for setting up factories in keeping with the promotional policy of the Indian government.[6]

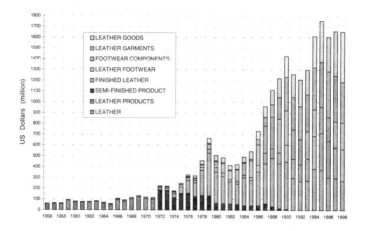

Sources: Council for Leather Exports (export in rupees), Economic Survey (exchange rate)

FIGURE 1: EXPORT OF LEATHER AND LEATHER
PRODUCTS FROM INDIA (1956–7 to 1998–9)

[6] The State Industries Development Corporation (SIDCO) is meant for small enterprises and the State Industries Promotion Corporation of Tamil Nadu Limited (SIPCOT) deals with medium- and large-scale industries. Their objective is industrialization of the more underdeveloped zones of Tamil Nadu. For this, they propose sites with the necessary infrastructure (roads, levelled ground, water, electricity) and also offer building loans, as well as tax benefits during the first few years. Most states have such development organizations, although the names differ.

Entrepreneurial Model

Profile of a Local Self-Made Man

With the sudden development and expansion of the leather industry in north Tamil Nadu, the Labbai Muslims acquired the reputation of being dynamic businessmen. The portrait of a Labbai family of entrepreneurs in the second half of the nineteenth century (Dupuis, 1969) has all the characteristics of a successful social model, which is still valid for today's entrepreneurs. In the middle of the nineteenth century, Muthu Meera Rawther was one of the first Muslims to take up leather trade and tanning. Proprietor of two factories in 1870, he was one of the richest merchants of Madras. At this time, Jamal Mohidin Rawther, Muthu Meera Rawther's nephew, left his village in north Tamil Nadu and joined his uncle in the capital. The industrialist gave his daughter in marriage to him and also took him into his prosperous business. But the nephew's—and new son-in-law's—inherent spirit of independence made him decide to start his own brokerage business. After a difficult start, by the beginning of the twentieth century, he had become one of the richest entrepreneurs in the leather business and had acquired several tanneries in Tamil Nadu. His descendants dominated the leather market in Madras until the end of the 1960s. His grandson, whose influence extended beyond Tamil Nadu, helped to set up the CLRI in Madras in 1953. This legendary model was built on the paradoxical articulation of family (or community) solidarity and entrepreneurial individualism.

Rawther (J.M.)

Businessmen who have built the largest shoe-manufacturing groups have charted very different courses. However, the same liberal logic of emancipation and independence characterizes their trajectories. One of them founded his first enterprise in the mid-1960s, after having been an accountant in a leather business in Madras. The other, who was a functionary in an export promotion council, started his group at about the same time by making use of contacts established abroad while on an exploratory mission. In the next generation, during the 1970s, there are many that launch their own enterprises independently

Self-made Men

of their fathers-in-law. There appears to be a difference of status among founders who were self-made men, together with their direct descendants, and the sons-in-law who launched their own independent businesses with their help. Whereas the latter perceive their enterprise as an autonomous family-owned industrial entity, the direct heirs of the pioneers consider them as a sort of extension of their own family. This shows that the model of the self-made man is highly valorized, as a result of which some entrepreneurs continue to exercise social domination over others.

Itinerary of a Business Executive

The entrepreneurial model is preferred by business executives, usually distant relatives of the proprietor, who seek to break free of their subordinate position. Nothing is more important than to shed the employee status, as is illustrated by the career of a young factory owner. After finishing college, Yussuf found employment in the maintenance and service division of a big shoe factory of Tholpuram. Some months later he was appointed head of the division. Communal solidarity probably had something to do with his appointment and rapid rise, for his father, who had died very early, had himself been an important tanner of the town. After five years, Yussuf resigned and started his own business in Madras. He purchased semi-finished leather, which he then processed by giving it out on job work to tanneries in Tholpuram, before selling the finished leather to shoe factories. It was necessary for Yussuf to constitute a reliable and diversified network of salesmen, tanners, and clients. In addition, it was his responsibility to procure all the tanning materials, for the tanner only supplies equipment and labour. Here is where the role of the community came in. Some distant relatives, whom Yussuf calls cousins, allowed him to make use of their commercial networks, taught him the tricks of the trade, thus protecting him from the fatal errors of inexperience. The role of the community is limited to this aspect. The cousins did not lend money. Islam proscribes loans on interest. Moreover, the risk of lending money to someone just starting out is too great. Fluctuations in purchase and selling prices can result in sudden and fatal reverses. Within one year, Yussuf was bankrupt. But his fall was cushioned by community solidarity. He went back to the factory where he got his old job back. Immediately he opened a soft drinks outlet with a partner. After one and a half years, he gave up this not very distinguished activity to launch a shoe accessories business (such as laces or rivets), supplying to some Tholpuram factories. Along with this he opened a workshop for assembling shoe uppers on a job-work basis. Yussuf continued to work in the factory, while the evenings and weekends were spent looking after the workshop. His partner had no secondary source of income other than this business. This time Yussuf wants to be really sure that the new venture will succeed before resigning from his job and becoming a full-time factory owner.

MUSLIM ETHIC AND SOCIAL PATRONAGE

According to the precepts of Islam, accumulated wealth must benefit the community through acts of solidarity. These are defined by the Koranic law (Shariah), which categorizes the forms of donation and services, as well as the recipients. There is however a concentric hierarchy of solidarity: in the centre is the immediate family, then the extended family, thirdly the community and lastly the city. The forms of donation or service are four in number. *Sadqa* is charity meant for the poor. *Zakat* is the payment of 2.5 per cent of a person's annual income: it is left to the donor to choose the mode of payment, which can eventually be administered by the mosque's board. *Khairath* involves all forms of donation and aid not specifically meant for the needy. Lastly, *hasnath-e-jaria* includes all the actions in favour of the people of the community and/or the city. *Muslim Ethic*

The rules of solidarity that apply to social patronage come under the *hasnath-e-jaria*. It is said in the Koran that for each person benefiting from such acts, God will reward the donor in the afterlife. It could be the construction of a school, a marriage hall, a mosque, a hospital, or a water reservoir. The bigger enterprises of the city generally have a social welfare department that provides free health services for the poorer sections living near the factories. Factory owners also participate in the various health and social development programmes organized in the town, such as camps where examination of eyes and surgery are performed free, vaccination campaigns, literacy drives. *Social Patronage*

STRUCTURE AND DYNAMICS OF
THE INDUSTRY

THE INDUSTRIAL DISTRICT

Concen-
tration of
Firms

From the nineteenth century onwards, the leather industry has been developed through a structure of industrial districts. This structure is characterized by a heavy concentration of firms dealing with the same industrial activity. It is also characterized at the same time by competition as well as cooperation between firms, induced by community solidarity and family linkages between proprietors (Cadène and Holmström, 1998). In the 1960s and 1970s, during the last phase of industrialization, the phenomenon intensified. While the concentration increased in certain specific zones, other less important zones virtually disappeared. Today, the concentration is found in two places: the business district in Chennai, and production centres in the north of the state, along the Palar River, and a bit in the suburbs of Chennai.

Central-
ization of
Head-
quarters

The headquarters of the leather industries in north Tamil Nadu are mostly located in the Periamet area of Chennai. This strategic location between the port and the main railway station was developed at the turn of the twentieth century. Initially, brokerage of leather and hides constituted Periamet's principal activity. Today, it also houses ancillary industries (such as manufacturing equipment, tanning materials, dealers in second-hand machines, especially to small enterpreneurs who are just starting out), information bureaus (leather publications), and organizations such as the All India Skins Hides Tanners Merchants Association, or the Council for Leather Export, which sometimes also provide logistical assistance to young entrepreneurs.[7]

Special-
ization of
Factories

Manufacturing units along the Palar river are characterized by hyper-technological specialization, each restricting its activity to a single product. Initially, one of these towns specialized in the tanning of sheepskins, another (Tholpuram) in goatskins,

---

[7] For example, the Council for Leather Export has placed its web site at the service of enterprises so that they can get orders.

and two others in cattle hides. But in the course of the final phase of industrialization, each town concentrated on a specific product. The first one limited itself to its traditional activity and therefore small tanneries were a permanent feature of the cityscape. One of the last followed a similar scenario but did go in for a little diversification by branching out into a side activity, namely the recuperation and processing of animal flesh for the gum industry. The other one owed its recent industrialization to industrial organizations like SIDCO and SIPCOT that have promoted the expansion of an industrializing industry in diverse sectors (chemicals, machines, leather and so on).

Tholpuram has been following a strategy of vertical integration, from tanneries to the shoe industry, with two types of products: shoe uppers and the full shoe. All the goods produced are exported to the United States and Europe (Denmark, Germany, Britain, Italy). Goatskin is used for shoe lining (inside part of the shoe). Thus, part of the leather produced in the Tholpuram tanneries is used by factories for the local market, but the major share is exported to the USA and Europe. Cowhide used for the outer shoe is generally imported from the United States and Latin America, because the quality of leather in India is not good enough. Today, the town has about thirty factories producing shoes. Thirteen large-scales ones employ some 500 to 800 people. But they are owned by four groups only, some of which also have factories in towns adjoining Tholpuram, and in Chennai and Bangalore. The biggest group employs nearly 3,000 people in its three Tholpuram factories, and more than 6,000 people in total, with a big tannery in Tholpuram, a factory in Chennai and one in Bangalore. The smallest of the four employs about 1,000 people. A dozen medium-sized firms employ between 100 and 200 people each. Lastly, a few small units (perhaps around sixty, but it is difficult to say with any degree of accuracy) have a staff of twenty to fifty people. These units depend entirely on bigger factories for job work, i.e. assembling leather pieces. Thus, a factory that employs 800 people, provides work for 1,200 outside people, if we count the approximately thirty job-work units that work exclusively for it.

Tholpuram

FAMILY RATIONALE OF CAPITAL MANAGEMENT

Kinship

The production site is above all the 'home' of the entrepreneurs, where the greater part of the family continues to live in a joint family (see pp. 24–9). In Chennai, most are nuclear families, though they reiterate their preference for an extended family and the solidarity that it represents. The head of the firm is also the head of the family. He bears responsibility for the family's financial well-being, its standing in the town, and the possibilities of expansion through marriage alliances. At Tholpuram, the prominent families are all connected by marriage (see Figure 2). In fact, all the entrepreneurs of this town dealing in leather are either closely related or connected, but a hierarchy is formed depending on the degree of the family's prosperity. Criteria for the selection of spouses are fixed on the basis of the social rules of marriage among south Indian Muslims and, in the case of industrial families, by the crucial factor of the handing down and future of capital from one generation to the next.

Marriage

The rules governing marriage, as we have already seen, are: (1) endogamy, that is to say marriage within the Labbai community; (2) isogamy (marriage into a family of equivalent social status) which is the practice in south India—here this is expressed by equal wealth; (3) the possibility of marriage with a cross cousin or a parallel cousin. Contrary to the Hindu model, marriage with a maternal uncle is considered incestuous.

Inheritance

The rules of inheritance are prescribed by the Shariah. Sons as well as daughters inherit from their parents. If the father dies intestate, male heirs inherit two-thirds of the assets, and the females one-third. But during his lifetime, the father can divide his worldly goods as he pleases. The woman remains the owner of her personal assets after her marriage (she takes them with her if there is a divorce), but they are managed by her husband. Thus the husband may be the head of the firm, but in reality he is only the manager of his wife's wealth. In the case of an heiress, the family's problem is to choose a son-in-law who will be capable of fructifying his wife's share of the wealth and ensuring the prosperity of the descendants.

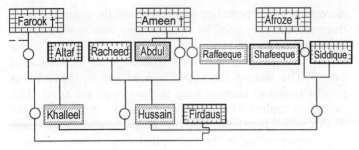

Network of kinship amongst the
main leather company managers in Tholpuram

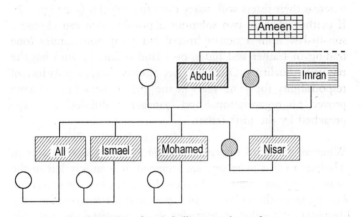

Strategies of capital alliance and transfer

KEY

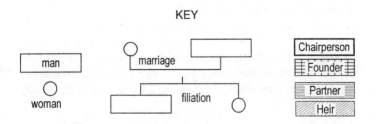

FIGURE 2: NETWORK OF KINSHIP AND STRATEGIES OF
CAPITAL ALLIANCE

Son-in-law   According to the prevailing social rules and the stakes involved, three strategies are possible: first, marriage into another Labbai industrial family of equal financial status. Marriage is thus a means of expanding the business through an association of capital. The second alternative is marriage with a cross or parallel cousin in order to keep the money in the family. This strategy is applied when the young woman inherits substantial wealth, which the family wants to safeguard, or when no young man corresponding to the first option can be found. Thus, in some families, the men may marry women from other families of the town, sometimes even from outside the Labbai community in the name of Islamic egalitarian and universal precepts, whereas their sisters will marry their first cousins (see Figure 2). If neither of these two solutions is possible, one can choose a son-in-law from a non-industrial but prosperous family (one trading in leather and hides, or a landed family) who has the requisite qualities. Often he has already held a position of responsibility for some years in the girl's father's firm. Having proved his organizational and managerial abilities, he is approached by the girl's father.

Daughter-in-law   Whereas the firms operate from the Periamet offices, it is in Tholpuram that marriages are arranged. It is mostly left to the women to make the final decision. If the head of the enterprise has learnt of the existence of a potential daughter-in-law (the daughter of another industrialist or an associate), he will rely on his wife or his mother to make the final choice. In any case, the onus of selecting her daughter-in-law is the future bridegroom's mother's responsibility.[8] Once the decision has been taken and the assent of the future in-laws obtained, the marriage settlement is negotiated by the men. It seems that capitalist strategies in the long term correspond to marriage strategies, which partly depend on the power of decision held by the women of the family. But in the short term, the firm's balance sheet constitutes a sort of social barometer of the family

---

[8] Accompanied by close relatives (sisters, married daughters, and elder sons' wives), she visits the houses of young marriageable girls to meet them and make her choice. The practice of *purdah* prevents any man—including the father of the girl—from accompanying them.

and determines the choice of marriage strategies. If a businessman who is looking for a suitable groom for his daughter incurs heavy losses unexpectedly at this stage, the chances are that he will not be able to make the sort of marriage alliance he would have wanted. The narrowness of the social circle and the extensive inter-marrying that goes on facilitates a permanent and collective surveillance of the families and their businesses, on the basis of which the choice is made.

Partnership

Marriage strategies structure relationships of cooperation and of competition between enterprises. Kinship supposes a close-knit solidarity with mutual exchange of various types of service (e.g. free loan of machines, of tanning materials, bus services for workers to and fro from work). This solidarity is especially decisive when choosing suppliers and subcontractors. When the shoe factory is not supplied with leather from its own group's tannery, it buys leather from a close relative by marriage or a son-in-law (most likely a family tannery willed to the daughter of the head of the firm). The same is true of shoes given out on job work for assemblage (sticking and sewing the pieces). The work will first be subcontracted to relatives. Often the latter (nephews, sons-in-law) will have already worked in the family firm for several years, before branching out on their own, probably with inputs in terms of advice and networks from the relative-cum-ex-employer. To some this method offers the advantage of training and also the guarantee of orders, which can be crucial in the initial stages. To others it means the formation of a reliable network of subcontractors, thanks to which they can delegate, if necessary, a substantial part of their production. But this solidarity also carries considerable risks. Taking the orders for granted, some subcontractors with little managerial experience adopt a wait-and-watch policy because they are not able to anticipate seasonal fluctuations or not able to manage within the small margins that the giver of orders leaves them.[9] Family solidarity here has reached its limits. True, it helped the son-in-law, the nephew or the brother-in-law to

---

[9] Out of Rs. 25 that a shoe upper may cost a 'giver of orders', he gives Rs. 5 to the job worker who assembles the shoe. From this Rs. 5, the job worker has to deduct his investments, pay his labour and procure the materials (thread and adhesives).

find their feet in the initial stages, but after that they are expected to fend for themselves and face the competition and market constraints that are part of the game. This attitude is another facet of this entrepreneurial model, based on the articulation of both individualism and community solidarity.

CONFLICTS AND INTERNAL RULES

All disputes and litigation involving members of the Labbai and Deccani communities are sorted out, as far as possible, by the regulatory bodies of the Muslim community, thus avoiding recourse to external arbitration.[10]

Muthuvelli Family conflicts pertaining to inheritance, divorce, etc., fall within the purview of the administrator of the mosque (*muthuvelli*) and his advisers. The members of the mosque's advisory board are residents of the area who have been co-opted on the basis of their devoutness in observing religious forms, and probity. The board elects a *muthuvelli* from among its members or from outside, who is the administrative and moral head of the 'parish' (*jamaat*). Among other things, he is responsible for preparing the budget and ensuring the mosque's prosperity. Conflicts within a family or between families are placed before him in his role of conciliator.[11] In the case of divorce, he intervenes as conciliator and, if his mediation does not succeed, he then pronounces judgement. The *muthuvelli* is not always from outside the world of business. At Tholpuram, the three *muthuvellis* from the residential areas where most industrialists and leather brokers live are themselves heads of firms. Two of them are among the town's more prominent industrialists. Their busy schedule forces them to delegate most of the day-to-day business to the board members, but, as holders of judicial and administrative power, they intervene directly in the more important and delicate matters in the life of the *jamaat*.

---

[10] Conversely, the Hindus generally apply to the civil courts for arbitration.

[11] In an industrial family of Tholpuram, a conflict over inheritance which was taken directly to court, went on for generations in an interminable series of sterile court cases, only to finally find a solution in the judgement pronounced by the *muthuvelli*.

In all instances of conflict, the community first appeals to its own politico-religious bodies to arrive at a solution. The same is done with industrial matters. In the mid-1990s, as a result of major pollution hazards, tanners from Tholpuram and other close-by industrial towns, were forced by the High Court to set up common plants for the treatment of chemical effluents, or to face closure of the tanneries. This obliged the tanners to discuss the re-location of these plants in the city and their financing. The sites selected compelled some of them to close down. The financial contributions that tanners were expected make also caused conflict. The secretary of the tanners' association, who was later appointed chairman of the treatment plant, acted as mediator. He was also the right hand man of the Tholpuram *qazi*. The *qazi* is the first dignitary of the town's Muslim community. Administrator and magistrate, he is the keeper of the law (Shariah). The *muthuvellis* of each mosque, in their role of advisers, confer with him about the administration of the community, management of the *wakf* (donations given by individuals to the community) and settlement of administrative and juridical questions outside the purview of the *jamaats*. The *qazi* of Tholpuram is 90 years of age. His right hand man (who is neither a *muthuvelli* nor the adviser of any *jamaat)*, has been invested with his powers and manages most of the affairs in his place and in his name. Thus, in a crisis situation involving the city's industrialists, the *qazi* intervenes *de facto* through his deputy to settle internal conflicts and arbitrate on matters that might otherwise lead to litigation. By setting up bodies that mediate and arbitrate, the religious space provides a privileged setting for structuring and regulating all aspects of social life, based on the primacy of the family. Once again, it forms the keystone of the local socio-economic edifice in which industrial activity is enshrined.

Qazi

INDUSTRIAL STRATEGIES AND PRODUCTION LOGIC

For the Western 'giver of orders' or buyer, the system of subcontracts forms the substratum of their professional relationship with the Indian shoe industry. It is characterized by intense technological specialization and limited production capacity. The largest Tholpuram firms work with a limited number of clients, often three or four and sometimes just one.

Contract   The process of drawing up a contract is divided into three stages of a total duration of roughly six months. During the first stage (of three months), the client sends a prototype of the shoe. The Indian manufacturer makes a sample, which he then returns to the client for approval. The latter checks the product and specifies the corrections that need to be made. The manufacturer then sends a second modified sample, and if this is approved, the contract is signed. The second stage (of two months) consists of spelling out the requirements and ordering leather from the tanneries. The third stage (one month), is the production [12] and delivery stage.

Principal   The increase both in production capacity and in flexibility, enabling the manufacturer to meet the increasing diversity of orders, is accomplished by giving out the less qualified jobs to subcontractors. Three or four big enterprises thus assume the status of 'giver of orders' in relation to a plethora of small units in the vicinity. Some demand that the subcontractor work exclusively for them in order to ensure high-quality work. Hence, these small units may be sure of getting orders, but their existence depends on the 'giver of orders'. On the other hand, for subcontracting units working with several clients, business is uncertain and there are periods, long or short, when they may have no orders.

Subcontract   In situations which are not under the control of the original client, the job-work chain can go down to two or three levels below the first contractor. For instance, Romeo, an Italian industrialist, subcontracts his shoes to 'Deccan Shoes', an important Bangalore manufacturer. 'Deccan Shoes' in turn subcontracts the production of shoe uppers to Ahmed, a small Tholpuram manufacturer who employs eighty people. Ahmed accepts more orders than he can handle. He keeps a part of the order for himself and gives out the rest to Shafee as well as to three other units that each employ fifteen to twenty people. But Shafee finds that plaiting the thongs adorning the shoe uppers is a manual operation that takes up too much of his

[12] One product line can range between 250 to 5,000 pairs of shoes. A factory with 1,000 employees produces about 2,500 pairs of complete shoes in a day, that is about 62,000 a month.

unit's time. He therefore decides to entrust this operation to his workers to do as overtime. The latter do part of it, and give the rest to the women of their family (sisters, cousins, mothers, aunts) and to women neighbours. The last and fourth level of job workers for Romeo is thus families of the workers of small units. But when Romeo comes to inspect the production, it is disastrous. The accumulation of subcontracts is synonymous with poor quality and a very high rate of defects. Two out of three pieces are rejected. Recent competition from neighbouring countries (China, Indonesia, Bangladesh), after the euphoria of the 1980s, has added to this new and critical situation. The second half of the 1990s imposed an industrial and marketing logic for which all firms were not prepared. The desire to make a fast buck led many to resort systematically to job work instead of developing an industrial strategy, which would enable them to fulfill their potential and meet their orders. Tholpuram industrialists justify the breakdown of the initial contract by stressing community solidarity that strengthens the client–supplier relationship. The 'givers of orders' recall their own small beginnings and reiterate their desire to help newcomers to succeed. On their part, the small units hope to grow in the wake of the big groups and match them one day. As soon as they reach the critical size enabling them to produce 500 pairs of shoes per day, these units reproduce the job-work scenario, descending to lower levels of work, but rising that much more in the local business and family hierarchies. Thus, social ambition and lack of real managerial skills encourage them to come up with schemes which give short-term benefits without any long-term planning. To avoid this dark scenario, the biggest shoe companies dealing directly with the international market demand that their subcontractors work exclusively for each of them. In this way, they are able to control the process and to insure quality production.

On their part, large-scale firms try to get rid of the sub-contractor status. Indian industrialists consider the dependence on Western clients as a repetition of the colonial situation. The more dynamic among them intend to position themselves directly on the international shoe market without any intermediaries. This independence is part of the initial logic underlying vertical integration strategies followed by business

Vertical Integration

firms since the modernization of tanneries: semi-finished leather → finished leather → shoe uppers → whole shoe. The new phase corresponds to the development of shoe prototypes as part of the new business procedure. Design teams working in groups of two to three technicians are trained at the CLRI. Samples are made with the help of foreign consultants and designers who inform companies about fashion trends and market openings in their own country. Firms take part in international leather fairs like those at Milan, Frankfurt, and Hong Kong to show their product range and get orders. Their entry into this market and their independent status does not seem to have changed the export destinations. However, it enables firms to work with clients who are dealing in other products besides shoes and to get massive orders from large-scale distributors and buying houses.

Joint Ventures

Lastly, a few industrialists plan their strategy on the basis of foreign collaboration. This option is however a marginal one in this industry. There are only two joint ventures at Tholpuram. The first, a large-scale one, employs 1,000 people. It was created in 1979 with a big American shoe industrialist. It produces day-wear and sports shoes of medium quality (priced from Rs. 3,000 to 4,000) under the brand name of the American partner. The latter held 35 per cent of the capital. On the Indian side, the capital came as a result of the self-sufficiency achieved by a part of the group's operations, at that time the biggest in Tholpuram. The magnate had in fact given his second daughter in marriage to one of his brilliant executives, with a university degree in commerce, from a prominent family of landlords of Tholpuram. In 1979, on the eve of the expansion of the shoe industry in Tholpuram, the son-in-law had suggested to the father-in-law that American exports be separated from the rest of the group's operations, in particular the business generated by the big American buyer. He then formed his own group, which included several factories, the joint venture constituting the principal one. This factory was fully independent, thanks mainly to a 100 per cent subsidiary located in the vicinity, which manufactured the synthetic and metallic components (such as soles, rivets, and laces). Today, the entire staff is Indian. The American partner's role is limited to management control from a distance. This joint venture is certified as ISO9000. The second joint venture, a 'medium scale' one, had 400 workers. It was set up at the beginning of the industrial boom in 1985, with a German partner who held 40 per cent of the equity. It manufactured up-market casual footwear, sold by mail order in Germany and some neighbouring countries. The two partners met through another prominent Tholpuram industrialist, a big exporter to Germany, who had been approached to set up a medium-sized joint venture which he was not interested in. His son-in-law, who is also his sister's son, was managing a small group consisting of a tannery and a small shoe factory, but with no real strategy or motivation. The industrialist suggested that the younger man seize this opportunity and the joint venture was set up. Today, responsibility of the management in the medium term is divided between the Indian proprietor (requirement estimates) and the German partner (choice of materials and their origin). A German technical manager handles production and the day-to-day operations. The rest of the staff is Indian. The enterprise has decided to concentrate on quality under the guidance of the German expatriate, in order to obtain the ISO9000 label. However, despite the apparent success of these two joint-ventures set up in the initial stages of the shoe boom, and despite the advantages offered by the formula (access to a much coveted market, though unknown and uncertain, certainty of recovering the initial investments, etc.), this type of collaboration is not much in demand. Other entrepreneurs are critical of it, as they feel that it reduces liberty of action and acts as a brake on new initiatives. Entrepreneurial individualism and its social implications in the joint spheres of the family and the community are still not reconciled to the control exercised by the partner or to joint-management. These are treated as inopportune intrusions that go much beyond the simple business context.

MANAGEMENT TRAINING

Industrialists play an active role in promoting general education till the Higher Secondary level, followed by higher studies. They encourage and finance Muslim educational societies that administer schools and colleges, which in theory are open to all but where most students are Muslims. Such societies go back

Professional Training

to the political activism of Muslim communities at the beginning of the twentieth century. Muslims generally had a very poor level of education and were dominated both by the British and by high-caste Hindus, who monopolized jobs in the administrative and teaching spheres. This social-reform movement was, firstly, a response to the British literacy programme, which was seen as a threat to the communitarian identity and, secondly, an attempt to be free from Hindu social domination. Today, Muslim educational societies offer programmes for the development and encouragement of all, independently of religious affiliation. But the fountainhead of this egalitarian discourse is nevertheless the Koran and Islam. One of the primary objectives is to raise the educational level of the Muslim community, statistically less inclined towards modern Western studies than Hindus. The industrial transformation that has taken place since the 1970s was accompanied by an improvement in the educational level of the new businessmen. Generally speaking, business initiation was done through hands-on training within the family or the community, after a more or less brief period of schooling. Tanners, for example, often drop out of school after the tenth standard, or after technical courses. In the case of industrialists, the general educational level is higher. Many of them pursue technical or commercial studies for two years after completely higher secondary schooling.

Studies Abroad

The third and last generation of shoe industrialists is still in the gestation stage. Most have studied abroad, particularly in the USA, after having attended the best schools in Chennai. Their higher studies are average. Most of them do not go beyond a Bachelor of Business Administration. Here again we can see the propensity to imitate an innovator or an achiever. Sending children abroad for study is a trend initiated by one businessman and immediately copied by all the others. For example, conformism induces them to send their progeny one after another to the same university after having sent them to the same school. One would expect higher studies to bring about a change in the managerial practices through the introduction of new models. However, these studies do not go very far and are not enough to produce full-fledged management professionals. In reality, the studies in themselves are of secondary importance.

The son is sent abroad to gain experience of 'Western culture' and its inner motivations, so that he may be able to understand the 'Western way of thinking'. Back in India, at the helm of affairs, he will be in a better position to understand the clients' requirements and to respond to them. In the world of shoe manufacturers, young magnates who have lived abroad constitute a sort of aristocracy compared to their elders, who have had to bear the responsibility of the enterprise directly. The latter are strongly in favour of the traditional model rather than the one that is progressively replacing it.

LIFE AND MANAGEMENT OF THE ENTERPRISE

INSIDE, OUTSIDE: TOWN, FACTORY AND SOCIETY

The management of shoe factories should be seen in the context of the recent industrialization of this sector and the social and cultural upheavals that this metamorphosis has brought in its wake. The city of Tholpuram, where the greater part of this study was conducted, now has 1,00,000 inhabitants, of whom approximately 50 per cent are Muslims, 25 per cent SC and 25 per cent Shudras and Vaishyas. The leather industry is the driving force of the economy. Today it employs between 18,000 and 20,000 people in the town and neighbouring villages. Apart from the factories, all professional activities and the structure of employment reflect the structure and rules of society.

Tholpuram

The professional specialization of castes and communities allots specific activities to individuals, which they are supposed to perform (see pp. 33–6). Tanneries also function on the basis of this social order and its hierarchical principles. The degrading tasks, such as desalting hides, shearing, and skinning are left to Scheduled castes. Muslims perform the more qualified tasks. A few Hindus from the dominant castes of the region (Mudaliyar, Vaniyar, Chettiar), who have studied at the CLRI, are sometimes recruited for these more qualified tasks (laboratory work, technical management, and so on) when proprietors do not find specialized personnel among their own community. The

Hierarchy of Job

managerial staff is exclusively Muslim, or nearly so, and always masculine, with women being employed as labour.

Women Employment

The increase in the number of shoe factories caused another major upheaval with the massive recruitment of women. Today, the number of women employed is two to three times higher than that of men; 80 per cent are Hindu, whereas 80 per cent of the men are Muslim. Muslim men fill all the managerial and administrative posts as executives, supervisory staff, etc., though some may be workers. Women are employed as labour. The entry of women into the factory has repercussions that are not limited to the work situation or to the professional context, for the division between public and private, which is very marked in the West, is not as strict in India (see pp. 26–9). Such radical changes in the sphere of work have had major repercussions on the entire social structure. Proprietors and factory managers held responsible for these social upheavals are sensitive to the severe criticisms levelled at them, especially by many of the political and religious leaders of the town—Hindu as well as Muslim. Gender intermixing at work is in fact the cornerstone of the social criticism of factories.

Women, Factories and Society

'Working in factories means that the woman leaves the house, that she is seen by strangers, that she is in contact with individuals from different backgrounds, interactions that cannot be monitored by the family. Now, the fact of young women, married or unmarried, working in a masculine environment everyday is against social rules and regulations' (Venou, 1999). This whole situation is particularly problematic for Muslim women in *purdah*, as direct contact is normally limited to male members of their immediate family. Outside the house they have to wear the veil and the *burqa*. But in the factory they have to work alongside men with their faces uncovered. In the early 1970s, when the first shoe factory was set up with an exclusively feminine work force and an exclusively masculine managerial staff, vehement protests by trade unions were taken up in mosques by leaders of Islamic religious movements, such as the Tabligh-i Jamaat and the Jamaat-i Islami. The employer who was under attack retorted that the women employed were of low status, poor or widows, and the employment offered to them was a form of charity enabling them to better their lot in life. In the ensuing decade, despite repeated protests from religious leaders, employment in factories became common. This situation has affected women's status within the family and in society. They now had a regular income, often higher than that of other members. In certain cases, this salary was even the family's only source of income. In society, the 'risk' of love marriages that contact between men and women in the workplace encourages, is the principal argument used by society to accuse women workers for their 'loose morals'. Love marriages lead to the emancipation of the couple from the constraints of the joint family and the solidarity that structures it (see pp. 19–32). Love marriages often imply an intercaste, or worse, an interreligious marriage.[13]

The social group in the factory tries to maintain its hold over individuals by keeping watch over the women workers, especially if the relatives and neighbours, who are also professional colleagues, find a particular relationship 'suspicious'. If necessary the family is informed, who then complains to the manager so that he may separate the individuals concerned. For his part, the head of the firm tries to give his factory an image of respectability by means of visible signs such as separate transport buses for men and women, or separate entrance/exit doors. Such practices are intended to convince religious leaders that *purdah* is observed in the factory, whereas the reality may be very different. Daily interaction between men and women results in a certain familiarity, which can even affect the relationship between the factory manager and the workers. However, the general attitude of suspicion with which the outside world regards social relationships within the factory compels those who work there to hide the reality of such relationships. If two colleagues of the opposite sex encounter each other on the street, they pretend not to know each other.

Monitoring Gender Inter-mixing

As opposed to tanneries where the workers are Scheduled castes, shoe factories generally have employees from different castes. The Scheduled Castes, Vaniyars and Mudaliyars (Shudras)

Hierarchy in Question

---

[13] Hindu extremists spread the rumour that, to meet the month's expenses, some women workers were invited for week-ends to the firm's guest house, situated outside the town, to entertain foreign buyers for the benefit of the Muslim boss.

are numerically dominant in the urban centres, and hence, not surprisingly, they constitute the largest group in factories. But many upper-caste men and women, such as the Chettiars and Acharis, are also employed. This situation implies a readjustment of the caste hierarchy associated with work and the introduction of new equations between caste members. With the exception of some individuals who keep their distance from Scheduled Castes, contact between castes in the work-place does not really constitute a problem as long as it does not lead to romance and love marriages with 'outcastes'. The internal organization of the industry thus gives rise to a new social situation in which sociability at work takes precedence over caste. Hindus and Muslims, executives and workers, eat at the same table and even share each other's food. However, beyond the confines of the factory the barriers are re-erected, and sometimes they come up even more rigidly for having been lowered at all, however briefly. Hindu heads of families often affirm the necessity of building their home in an 'acceptable' social environment that excludes Muslim neighbours.

MODALITIES OF RECRUITMENT

Recruitment in the Family

The recruitment of labour and managerial staff is determined more or less strictly by the rule of concentric circles of solidarity: close family, extended family, religious community, then town. The first circle of recruitment is thus the close and extended family. Operational jobs (such as factory manager, workshop manager, foreman) and the general administration of the factory are thus reserved for close (such as brothers, sons-in-law, first cousins) or distant relatives, whose level of education is not very important at this stage. On the other hand, their proximity to the factory owner greatly determines their career prospects. The very close relatives are given top jobs in the middle level hierarchy or in the administration, where they can familiarize themselves with the working of the firm. After this they rise in the hierarchy by getting 'hands on' training. Distant relatives are generally given less important posts, as ordinary workers or clerical staff. In the latter category, there is a possibility of them rising to the position of chief supervisor. The closeness of the family relationship with the owner also determines the degree of indulgence that the latter shows his relative in offering him the post. Some owners confessed that relatives could be quite useless in the firm, so much so that it would be more profitable to pay them a pension to remain at home. But a particular relationship with these employees (for example the son of the owner's elder brother) prevents this kind of step from being taken. On the other hand, the owner is more demanding with distant cousins after the initial gesture of offering them employment has been made (though, all things being equal, it is a relative rather than a non-relative who will be promoted). It is the same attitude which gives relatives preference over others as subcontractors and suppliers: it is then the responsibility of the beneficiary to take advantage of the initial start that has been given to him. Community solidarity does not oblige the factory owner to go beyond the first gesture. If offering a relative a job forms part of the prescribed rules of solidarity, the head of the firm expects the employee to give proof of his abilities to justify the promotion.[14] Technical skills acquired with experience are an important criterion; but the first requirement is complete devotion to the job, expressed by the phrase 'to work hard and sincerely'.

Recruitment within the Community

After the close and extended family, the Muslim community forms the second large circle of solidarity. It is this circle that some factory owners prefer to tap to recruit a factory manager with a degree (such as an engineer, B.A. or M.A. in Commerce, M.B.A.) rather than entrust management to a member of the family. However, most of these management professionals are natives of the town or related to one of its families. Their previous experience probably consisted of a managerial position in a firm or as head of a division in diverse sectors (aeronautics, banking, chemicals). It is from amongst the town's Muslim community that most of the male labour force and a part of the female labour force are recruited. Employment as a worker is obtained through recommendation. In most cases it is the candidate's close relative (father, mother, uncle, aunt, brother-in-law) who recommends him. This person is either an

[14] But we have seen that such a requirement is not always available in the restricted family circle, which continues to impose its own rules in the workplace, rules that the head of the enterprise has to accept.

employee in the factory, or a distant relative or an acquaintance of the proprietor's.

Recruitment of Women

The third circle of recruitment is situated outside the Muslim community, but within the town and neighbouring villages. It involves the majority of the women workers from the Hindu community. Women workers are preferred because they are more amenable to orders, more efficient and not interested in trade unionism. During the 1980s, the factory owners gave preference to their own community, but two reasons contributed to the employment of Hindu women. Firstly, the practice of *purdah* restricts Muslim women from working outside the home. Secondly, during the 1990s, the minimum level of education for employment was the tenth standard. This requirement penalized poor Muslim women, whose educational level was generally low, i.e. just till the fifth standard. Hindu women started to seek jobs out of economic necessity. The family sent one of its girls to the factory to earn some money and so broke the social taboo ('factory work encourages promiscuous relationships and love marriages'). The guarantee of a regular and relatively high income, in comparison with the family's normal income, finally prevailed over the taboos. Once she was employed, the young girl—or woman—found employment for her relatives and neighbours by recommending them to the factory manager. Thus, particular streets or zones are full of factory workers whereas others, of equivalent socio-economic status, are devoid of them. One of the reasons for female employment in factories is the need to collect a dowry in order to marry. Most women workers leave the factory once they are married. The poorer ones, however, continue to work after marriage. Their salary often constitutes the principal if not the sole income of the household, which could sometimes confer on them the status of implicit or explicit head of the family.

Recruitment of Specialists

Lastly, the Hindu community has traditionally followed certain professions, which are not generally taken up by Muslims. Most accountants are upper-caste Hindus; it is the same with some technical jobs in the field of design and development, necessitating technicians or engineers trained at the CLRI, or in the maintenance and service divisions.

MANAGEMENT AND STRUCTURE OF POWER

HEAD OFFICE

The firm functions on the basis of a centralized, family-controlled mode of management. Even in the Indo-American joint venture, managed by professionals, the group's chairman firmly believes in the primacy of the family in the overall management process. Claiming dissimilarity with other factories where the family model prevails, the Indian partner affirms the principle of 'controlled professionalism'. As in the more traditional family-owned enterprises, its control is seen as a guarantee of rationality in the organization's management. In all firms, decisions are taken at the head office, by the proprietor (the chairman of the group), the son and heir to the factory (the general manager), and the procurement manager (more often than not a close relative of the proprietor).

Centralized Decision Making

The chairman intervenes at all levels in the enterprise, from the group's strategy to the production workshops in the factory. On the one hand, he defines the overall policy and working of the group. He draws the guidelines for future growth, enlisting the support, if necessary, of the leather export-promotion councils on whose board he serves. On the other hand, he regularly monitors the running of the factories and the tanneries, visiting production units at least twice a week.

Chairmanship

The son manages the factory from the head office. His particular domain is marketing and client management. He also organizes production and is directly responsible for the recruitment of managerial staff and skilled workers. The father closely monitors his work. Strategic decisions—for example, the choice of diversification or reverting to a limited range of products—are always taken jointly with his parent.

Management (General)

The third most important figure in the head office is the procurement manager. Among other things, he is responsible for determining the requirements of leather and its purchase. This material accounts for over 60 per cent of a shoe's total cost. As a result, the procurement manager must be thoroughly

Management (Supplies)

familiar with his suppliers in order to avoid unpleasant surprises (e.g. bad quality leather, wrong interpretation of orders). Some procure leather only from their own tannery, but most only produce goat leather for lining. A small amount of cow or buffalo leather, for uppers, comes from a neighbouring town, but the supply is mainly from abroad (USA, Latin America, Europe). It is difficult to obtain information on the risks and guarantees involved in these transactions. In the case of imported leather, the transactions are normally guaranteed by a written contract. Where local leather is concerned, it is the control exercised by the family and the community that ensures the success of transactions. Also, the privilege of monitoring such a system remains with the head of the firm, on the basis of family and community linkages. He often operates from outside—for example, marriages are a perfect occasion for meeting and transacting business deals. So such matters are regulated by familial and socio-religious structures. Only this thorough knowledge seems capable of guaranteeing the quality of the product and its timely delivery. Within the enterprise, the procurement manager also has to exercise a strict control by centralizing purchase orders. In some firms he goes to the factory several days a week to supervise ongoing production.

Manage-
ment
(Factory)

The factory manager represents the central authority and sees to it that orders from above are obeyed. He is in charge of daily operations as well as administration and accounts. He may also have to see to it that the delivery schedule is respected.

FACTORY

Pyramid of
Command

The factory functions on the basis of a pyramidal organization of the Fayolian type, i.e. a functional and hierarchical division of work into units of command in which each person receives orders from one and only one hierarchical superior, relating to working hours, work methods, workload, etc. This leads to a compartmentalization of the social life of the production-shops, based on a strong sense of identity of individuals with their profession.

A careful observation of the hierarchical relations prevailing in the production-shops suggests that management's authority rests on two fundamental rules external to the production space. The compliance characteristic of women workers is based on the inferior social status assigned to them. We noticed for example that in several instances where difficult work situations gave rise to discontent among workers, women workers preferred to find a solution on their own rather than risk disturbing the foreman or the production-shop manager. 'It is always like this, even at home', they said. With regard to the men, the power exerted by the hierarchical superiors is framed in the mechanisms of solidarity pertaining to the family and the community. The terms of address are part of the register of kinship (see pp. 19–32). A hierarchical superior is respectfully addressed as 'brother' (*bhaiya*, or, for example, Ahmed *bhai*), or, depending on his age, the factory manager may also be called 'father'—a manager's wisdom, in one of the most important factories of Tholpuram, has earned him the title of 'master' (*hazrat*). These forms of address, highlighting the family connection or intimacy, is not limited to the Muslim community alone. Hindu women also use such terms that are generally associated with Muslims. (This is a characteristic of inter-community or interregional relationships at many levels in India.)

Staff Management

It is essential for company managers to respect and preserve the social mores. The factory manager plays an important role as guarantor of this social order *vis-à-vis* the factory owner. The unfortunate experiences of other neighbouring factories have shown that when this internal social order based on the endorsement of a collective family link is relaxed, trade unionism develops within the enterprise—or is injected from outside—and radically alters relationships by introducing the idea of class struggle. Hierarchical relationships then become conflict-ridden, criticism of working conditions and trade-union disputes turn into chronic work-to-rule strikes, and the entire organization rapidly reaches a state of chaos. To counter this risk, some factory managers promote a particular worker as leader to represent his colleagues. It is interesting to note how relations between the two are reduced to a father–son relationship, marked by paternalistic morality on the one side: 'Your

Paternalism

demands must be fair and reasonable',—and deference on the other: 'Our manager is a good man. Thanks to his good management, we have work the whole year round.'

MANPOWER PLANNING

Promotions   Opportunities for promotion are reserved exclusively for members of the family and the community, provided—as we have seen—that individuals earn this promotion through their diligence and technical abilities. Hindus are *a priori* excluded from promotion for posts at the top end of the factory hierarchy. They are hired for skills acquired through higher studies and previous professional experience, but very few of them can hope for some upward mobility in their career. In fact, the further one moves away from the proprietor's family circle, the fewer such opportunities are available. Promotion causes individuals to evince a lasting gratitude towards the hierarchical superior who has given them this chance. Thus, a system of clientelism develops, especially in the production units, which reinforces the relationship of command. At the lowest level, the existing hierarchy among workers, based on their performance (quantity and quality), sustains this clientelism. Each one is urged to rise in the hierarchy by putting in supplementary hours of work, which are allotted only to the best workers, or to those who are selected for promotion. Opportunities of rising in the hierarchy are extremely rare and career mobility in the factory context practically non-existent. Hence, conscious that they are stagnating in their present position, with no chance of promotion, many production shop-managers and foremen leave their jobs after fifteen to twenty years of service, in order to start their own units.

Promotion   Apart from this traditional system of hierarchy and individual
of Women   promotions, it is important to observe a more collective phenomenon that contributes to the redefinition of gender-based division of work and social hierarchies in jobs initially intended for men. Traditionally, women are given jobs inferior to those of the men. For example, in the 'cutting' section, the men operate the machines while the women 'helpers' sort out and arrange the cut pieces. But gradually managers realized that

women are not only as capable as the men at skilled jobs, but are in fact more efficient. One of the reasons for this rapid transformation is due to the quick turnover of the female workforce combined with the recent requirements for minimum educational qualification. One-third of the female workforce changes each year, whereas the educational level of the male workforce, initially recruited with an educational level generally below the third standard, remains relatively stable. Education provides workers with a capacity for conceptualization and abstraction of situations, which enables them to formulate hypotheses and develop their deductive faculties. Workers with little or no education are not capable of this. The opening of skilled jobs to women in the workshops is partly because of this intellectual ability, which has given them greater autonomy than their male colleagues and the capacity to take the initiative and directly resolve day-to-day problems at work.

The traditional models of hierarchy and promotion of workers are also undergoing change through the introduction of new management techniques (see also pp. 57–62). Some firms are laying increasing stress on human resource development by organizing training and coaching sessions for the personnel (workers and managerial staff) in order to develop team spirit and internal cohesiveness. The sessions are organized in the form of games to promote group dynamics and interactive seminars in which the participants are made to use key words and messages that the enterprise wants to valorize. The message of team cohesiveness contains the implicit notion of gender equality, transgressing traditional precepts and further widening the gulf between social norms within and outside the factory. The introduction of these new managerial techniques is partly due to the new generation of proprietors who are taking over management of the factories. But clients also play a leading role. We have seen earlier that these factories work with a limited number of buyers. The latter have considerable say in the production process and internal working of the firm. Clients committed to a long-term collaboration demand the incorporation of mechanisms guaranteeing quality, with special emphasis on manpower strategies. These mechanisms are structured along two main lines: first, the development of multiple skills enabling worker mobility from one work post to another and,

Management Remodeled

secondly, normalization of work procedures in order to increase standardization of production. These new measures give rise to discontent amongst the middle management, who can no longer exercise their old power over the workers. Technical expertise and clientelist motivations of those presently in power are losing ground with the new techniques of management and training of the workforce.

CONCLUSION

Culture plays a crucial role in the development of enterprises and their mode of management. Nevertheless, the dynamic nature of Labbai entrepreneurship, readily claimed by the community, is also the result of many external circumstances. The socio-political factors appear preponderant and individual innovations in this sector are few and far between. Some leaders who break away from traditional practices, or overturn them altogether, perhaps through indirect constraints such as those exercised by the Seetharamiah Committee (see p. 105), are the ones to initiate change. Around them, the majority's conservatism finds expression in its timorous reaction to innovations. But once the new model begins to offer all the guarantees of success, it opts for a conformist and massive reproduction of it.

With the advent of a new generation of managers, greater flexibility is observed with regard to the family and the community, and more importance is given to recruiting competent professionals. However, the latter are still selected as much as possible from the all-important spheres of family and community. In this context, the favouritism shown to relatives in the matter of jobs is now being questioned. But anyway, real management training takes place on the job, in the family business and under the father's authority, who sets the goals and the rules. Practices are very closely linked to family and community values. The process of change here is very rapid. It is not limited to the production space but also affects the structure of the surrounding society, and its traditional mechanisms of cohesiveness.

Henceforth, management is part of the agenda of social change. The principal upheaval caused by the factory is the creation of a space for sociability, which is gradually disassociating itself from the rest of society. The social rules that prevail within the work place are proscribed outside. This upheaval is caused by the confrontation of two social structures: a class structure introduced by industrialization and wages, and the old caste structure. It promotes conflict, in the sense that it encourages the questioning of the traditional social order. For all that, it does not imply the replacement of one structure by another, but rather their enduring co-existence.

Aware of the stakes involved, even if they are not conceived in these terms, industrial leaders are conscious that social cohesiveness inside the enterprise henceforth implies managerial action outside the factory. Such intervention takes the form of health and social programmes, described earlier. The Muslim ethic legitimizes this intervention and gives it its particular form. But beyond the cultural and religious dimensions, these actions seek to reduce the emerging social schisms. The dominant economic actors thus promote a local form of 'civic enterprise', responsible for piloting an inevitable change and giving it a desirable or at least an acceptable shape.

IV. Conclusion

During the industrial revolution in Europe, business and capital management played a crucial role in the development of the so-called 'modern' society. Max Weber's conception of 'modernity' is probably the most widespread: modernity comes from the rationalization of production practices and, more generally, of the political and economic management of society. Today modernity and globalization are closely linked (Giddens, 1992) to signify the permanent extension of rationalization and internationalization of social relationships. These relationships break loose from their local moorings and their cultural specificity to become part of a global process governed by two types of macro-systems. One falls within the realm of economics. It expresses itself through uniformization of the modes of creation and exchange of wealth (for example, the market economy or electronic money). The other is in the domain of politics. It corresponds to regulatory mechanisms playing a bigger and bigger role in the structuring societies (for example, the World Trade Organization or ISO standards).

These two systems of rationalization at the global level intervene at the local level by modifying lifestyles and social relationships, for instance, consumer habits, means of communication, access to information, forms of work. Thus, social relationships seem to be subordinated to the political and economic controls that act on and modify the cultural fundamentals. In India, this subordination to politics and economics is very real, as is very often illustrated in the history of the five big industrial families (see Chapter II). But this economics–politics *versus* social–cultural relationship can also be inverted, as the example of the Tholpuram leather industry demonstrates many times over (see Chapter III): forms of production and power are subordinated to the socio-religious systems that organize social relationships, define the possibilities of co-operation and determine the strategies; economic power is reinforced through the dominant position acquired in religious and family life that structure communities.

The above schematization must therefore be treated circumspectly. The groupings that we demarcate are not all obvious, and the same may be said of the cause-to-effect relationship that we commonly postulate. This is undoubtedly what India teaches us above all, with its extraordinary capacity to overturn our categories as much as to transform its own. In the midst of trade networks spanning several centuries, it did not in fact fail to quickly integrate behaviour, doctrines, ideas and values from elsewhere, especially from the West. Often, these foreign influences did not simply take the place of traditional concepts and practices. On the contrary, they were added to those already in place, forming intricately woven and sometimes surprising combinations. Or they co-existed with them, occupying a new sphere of existence in the peculiar relationship that India has with time, space, nature, machines, gods and money (see Chapter I).

To help us to understand Indian reality in another way, and bring it closer to ours, perhaps we could try and think in terms of 'greatness' and of 'worlds', as we are invited to do by Luc Boltanski and Laurent Thévenot in an essay on our societies (Boltanski and Thévenot, 1991). It thus no longer means associating a realm of values with groups of persons, as classical sociology often does, but on the contrary thinking that human beings—unlike objects—can fulfil themselves in different worlds. In this context, Boltanski and Thévenot distinguish six worlds, that is to say six cohesive and self-sufficient organizational ensembles of greatness. Greatness is how we express beings and things, how we embody them, how we understand them and how we represent them. Thus, a being or a thing can be 'small' in one world and 'great' in another. In the 'merchant world' for example,

People are in a state of 'smallness' when they do not produce utility, when they are *unproductive*, when they contribute little *work*, because of *absenteeism*, or excessive job *turn-over*, or because they are *inactive, unemployed, handicapped*, or because they produce bad quality work and are *inefficient*, unmotivated, *under-qualified, unsuitable*. Things are small when they are *subjective*. Human beings are also small when instead of setting their sights on the *future*, they remain anchored in the past, by not *evolving* enough, remaining *static*, rigid, *unsuitable*. (Boltanski and Thévenot, 1991: 254–5)

In the merchant world, people are therefore *separated* from each other (particularly from any domestic linkage), *free*, in such a way as to lend themselves willingly to any *transaction* that presents itself. In short, subjects are as *available* as goods on the *market*. (Ibid.: 248)

In the 'domestic world' on the contrary, or rather in the 'domestic city' from which this domestic world takes its inspiration,[1]

The greatness of people depends on their hierarchic position in a chain of personal dependence within a universe ordered by God, with ranks and grades [...]. The individual cannot, in this model, be separated from his membership of a community, which itself is conceived as a person characterized by a rank. He is himself defined by his lineage, which has its own identity, superior to that of the individuals who create it over time, so that the testator and the heir can rightfully be considered as one and the same person [...]. The individual is a link in the 'great chain of beings' and each finds himself wedged between a superior from whom he receives, through the medium of a personal relationship, the possibility of acceding to greatness, and inferiors whom he encompasses and embodies. In this domestic city, the link between human beings is conceived as the creation of a family linkage: each one is father to his subordinates and entertains a filial relationship with authority. But this analogy to the family refers not so much to blood relationships as to the fact of belonging to the same house, as territory in which the relationship of domestic dependence is rooted [...]. Human beings are distributed according to the relationship they have with [this] house [...], and, inside the house, according to their contribution to the reproduction of the lineage. This mode of distribution neutralizes the age gap since children distinguish themselves less from adults [...] than they oppose each other within the same domestic unit, depending upon whether they are the elder [...] or the younger, the latter being condemned to seek fortune away from home [...]. To know one's rank is to know one's greatness and to know oneself: the 'honourable man' [...] is appreciated for his capacity to not be unaware of what he is (which, in the logic of this city, is a sign of

---

[1] According to Boltanski and Thévenot, each 'common world' originates in a theoretical ideal, in a model of justice, a sort of political philosophy which, in the case of the domestic city (a description of which is produced here), is based on the analyses or citations of authors such as Auerback, Bloch, Bossuet, Claverie and Lamaison, Condorcet, de Bonald, Kantotowicz, La Bruyere, Mousnier, and Tocqueville.

madness) that is to say, the exactitude with which he is able to appreciate his greatness by ascribing it to the place he occupies in the chain of personal dependency. Even the servants, despite the misery that is their lot, share in their master's greatness and in his wealth. (Boltanski and Thévenot, 1999: 116–17)

This domestic city is of course a theoretical construction, a sort of philosophical caricature. But the resonance of its description with our sociology of the Indian businessman is striking. A major dissimilarity with India nevertheless remains. Our capacity to realize ourselves simultaneously in the merchant world and in the domestic world is very limited, for these two worlds are particularly conflict-ridden.

India, on the other hand, still tries to reconcile them, to not disassociate or oppose them.

APPENDICES

The Fifty Biggest Family-owned Groups according to Turnover (1995–6)

(turnover in crores of rupees)

No.	Houses	Turn.	Chairman	Community	HQ	Companies
1	Tata	31,471	Tata, R.N.	Parsi	Mumbai	TISCO, TELCO
2	Birla, B.K.–K.M.	11,422	Birla, B.K. and K.M.	Marwari, Maheshvari	Calcutta & Mumbai	Century Textiles, Grasim, Hindalco
3	Ambani	8,468	Ambani, D.H.	Gujarati	Mumbai	Reliance Industries
4	Goenka, R.P.	5,641	Goenka, R.P.	Marwari, Agarwal	Calcutta	Ceat, CESC, RPG Telecom, Spencers
5	Thapar, L.M.	3,984	Thapar, L.M.	Punjabi, Khatri	Delhi	Karam Chand Thapar & Bros., APR Ltd., Crompton Greaves
6	SPIC–MAC	3,896	Chidambaram, M.A.	Chettiar Nagarattar	Chennai	Tamil Nadu Petroproducts, MAC Industries, Manali Petrochemicals
7	Bajaj	3,771	Bajaj, Rahul	Marwari, Agarwal	Pune	Bajaj Auto, Bajaj Electricals, Maharashtra Scooters
8	M & M	3,472	Mahindra, Keshub	Punjabi, Khatri	Mumbai	Mahindra & Mahindra, Mahindra Ugine Steel, Mahindra Engg.
9	Birla, G.P.–C.K.	3,126	Birla, G.P.	Marwari, Maheshvari	Calcutta & Delhi	Hindustan Motors, Orient Paper, Hyderabad Indus
10	Escorts	2,865	Nanda, H.P.	Punjabi	Delhi	Escorts Automotives, Escorts JCB, Goetze

No.	Houses	Turn.	Chairman	Community	HQ	Companies
11	Jindal	2,770	Jindal, O.P.	Marwari	Delhi	Jindal Strips, Jindal Ferro Alloys, Shalimar Paints
12	Jumbo	2,693	Chhabria, M.R.	Sindhi	Dubai	Dunlop India, Falcon Tyres, Maharashtra Distilleries, Shaw Wallace
13	Kirloskar	2,667	Kirloskar, Vijay	Brahmin, Karhada	Bangalore	Kirloskar Bros., K. Copeland, K. Electric, KOEL, K. Pneumatic
14	Birla, K.K.	2,492	Birla, K.K.	Marwari, Maheshvari	Delhi	Hindustan Times, Gobind Sugar, Oudh Sugar, Chambal Fertilisers
15	UB	2,484	Mallya, Vijay	?	Bangalore	United Breweries, Best & Crompton, Mangalore Chemicals
16	Dhoot	2,482	Dhoot, Venigopal S.	Marwari	Mumbai	Videocon Appliances, V. Narmada Electronics, V.International
17	Murugappa	2,471	Subbiah, M.V.	Chettiar Nagarattar	Chennai	Carborundum Univ., Cholamandalam Inv., Tube Invests of India
18	Duncans	2,440	Goenka, G.P.	Marwari	Calcutta	Andhra Cements, Duncan Industries, NRC, Star Paper Mills
19	Mafatlal, A.	2,374	Mafatlal, Arvind	Gujarati, Patel	Mumbai	Gujarat Gas, NOCIL, Mafatlal Industries
20	Usha	2,227	Rai, Vinay	Punjabi, ?	Delhi	Usha India, Gordon Herbert, Information Technologies
21	BPL	2,148	Nambiar, T.P.G.	Malayali, Nair	Bangalore	BPL, BPL Engineering, BPL Refrigeration

No.	Houses	Turn.	Chairman	Community	HQ	Companies
22	Wadia	2,120	Wadia, Nusli	Parsi	Mumbai	Bombay Dyeing, AFCO Industrial, Bombay Burma Trading
23	MRF	2,011	Mappilai, K.M.M.	Syrian Christian	Chennai	MRF, Funskool
24	ISPAT	2,004	Mittal, M.L.	Marwari	Calcutta	Ispat Profiles, Ispat Alloys, Ispat Industries
25	Lalbhai	1,971	Lalbhai, Arvind	Gujarati, Jain	Ahmedabad	Arvind Mills, Atul, Cibatul, Amtrex Appliances
26	Singhania, H.S.	1,969	Singhania, H.S.	Marwari, Agarwal	Delhi	JK Industries, JK Corp., JK Pharma-chem, Central Pulp Mills
27	Siel	1,908	Shriram, Siddharth	Punjabi, Agarwal	Delhi	Shriram Honda Power Equipment, Shriram Pistons, Siel
28	Godrej	1,872	Godrej, S.P.	Parsi	Mumbai	Godrej Soaps, G. Hicare, Swadeshi Detergents
29	Hinduja	1,830	Hinduja, S.P.	Sindhi, Shikarpuri	London	Ashok Leyland, Hinduja Finance, Astra–IDL, Gulf Oil India
30	Williamson Magor	1,786	Khaitan, B.M.	Marwari	Calcutta	Bishnauth Tea, Eveready Industries, G. Williamson, India Foils
31	Lloyds	1,755	Gupta, Raj Narayan	Brahmin	Mumbai	Lloyds Steel Inds., Lloyds Metal & Engineers
32	Amalgamation	1,750	Sivasailam, A.	Brahmin, Tamil	Chennai	Amco Batteries, Bimetal Bearings, India Pistons, Simpson & Co.
33	Birla, M.P.	1,702	Birla, Priyamvada	Marwari, Maheshvari	Calcutta	Assam Jute, Universal Cables, Birla Corp.

No.	Houses	Turn.	Chairman	Community	HQ	Companies
34	Singhania, V.	1,694	Singhania, Vijaypat	Marwari, Agarwal	Mumbai	Raymond Synthetics, JK Chemicals, JK Helene Curtis
35	Torrent	1,665	Metha, Uttambhai	Gujarati	Ahmedabad	Ahmedabad Electricity, Surat Electricity, Torrent Cables
36	Birla, S.K.	1,578	Birla, Sudarshan K.	Marwari, Maheshvari	Calcutta	Birla VXL, Mysore Cements, Sidharth Soya Products
37	Ruchi	1,435	Shahra, K.C.	?	Indore	Ruchi Soya Industries, R. Strips & Alloys, Madhya Pradesh Glymchem
38	Indo Rama	1,397	Lohia, M.L.	Marwari	Delhi	Indo Rama Synthetics, Uniworth International, Woolworth
39	Dalmia, Sanjay	1,393	Dalmia, Sanjay	Marwari, Agarwal, Jain	Delhi	Bharat Explosives, Dalmia Cement, Gujarat Heavy Chemicals
40	Modi	1,357	Modi, Vinay Kumar	Marwari, Agarwal	Delhi	Modi Rubber, Modistone
41	Nagarjuna	1,341	Raju, K.S.	Raju	Hyderabad	Nagarjuna Fertilizers & Chemicals, Nagarjuna Steels
42	Apollo	1,289	Kanwar, Onkar S.	Punjabi, Sikh	Delhi	Apollo Tyres, Premier Tyres
43	Premji	1,287	Premji, Azim H.	Bohra Muslim	Mumbai	Wipro, Wipro Finance
44	Thapar, M.M.	1,234	Thapar, Man Mohan	Punjabi, Khatri	Delhi	JTC, JTC Electronics
45	Doshi, V.	1,226	Doshi, Vinod L.	Gujarati, Jain, Digambara	Mumbai	Premier Auto Electric, Walchandnagar Industries
46	Essar	1,214	Ruia, Sashi	Marwari	Mumbai	Essar Oil, Essar Shipping, Essar Steel, South India Shipping Corp.

No.	Houses	Turn.	Chairman	Community	HQ	Companies
47	Mukand	1,211	Shah, Viren J.	Gujarati	Mumbai	ISPL Industries, Mukand, Mukand Engineers
48	Kalyani	1,187	Kalyani, N.A.	?	Pune	Bharat Forge, Automotive Axles, Kalyani Brakes
49	Ranbaxy	1,182	Singh, Parvinder	Punjabi, Sikh	Delhi	Ranbaxy Drugs, Ranbaxy Laboratories, Solus Pharmaceuticals
50	NEPC	1,161	Khemka, Ravi P.	Marwari, ?	Chennai	NEPC India, NEPC Textiles, South India Cements

Source (turnover): *Business Today*, 'India's Business Houses 1947–1997', 22 Aug.–6 Sept. 1997.

APPENDIX 2

The Fifty Biggest Family-owned Groups according to Community (1995–6)

(turnover in crores of rupees)

No.	Houses	Turn.	Chairman	Community	HQ	Companies
I	MARWARI, MAHESHVARI	51,399				
2	Birla, B.K.–K.M.	11,422	Birla, B.K. and K.M.	Marwari, Maheshvari	Calcutta & Mumbai	Century Textiles, Grasim, Hindalco
4	Goenka, R.P.	5,641	Goenka, R.P.	Marwari, Agarwal	Calcutta	Ceat, CESC, RPG Telecom, Spencers
7	Bajaj	3,771	Bajaj, Rahul	Marwari, Agarwal	Pune	Bajaj Auto, Bajaj Electricals, Maharashtra Scooters
9	Birla, G.P.–C.K.	3,126	Birla, G.P.	Marwari, Maheshvari	Calcutta & Delhi	Hindustan Motors, Orient Paper, Hyderabad Indus
11	Jindal	2,770	Jindal, O.P.	Marwari	Delhi	Jindal Strips, Jindal Ferro Alloys, Shalimar Paints
14	Birla, K.K.	2,492	Birla, K.K.	Marwari, Maheshvari	Delhi	Hindustan Times, Gobind Sugar, Oudh Sugar, Chambal Fertilisers
16	Dhoot	2,482	Dhoot, Venigopal S.	Marwari	Mumbai	Videocon Appliances, V. Narmada Electronics, V. International
18	Duncans	2,440	Goenka, G.P.	Marwari	Calcutta	Andhra Cements, Duncans Industries, NRC, Star Paper Mills
24	ISPAT	2,004	Mittal, M.L.	Marwari	Calcutta	Ispat Profiles, Ispat Alloys, Ispat Industries

No.	Houses	Turn.	Chairman	Community	HQ	Companies
26	Singhania, H.S.	1,969	Singhania, H.S.	Marwari, Agarwal	Delhi	JK Industries, JK Corp., JK Pharmachem, Central Pulp Mills
30	Williamson Magor	1,786	Khaitan, B.M.	Marwari	Calcutta	Bishnauth Tea, Eveready Industries, G. Williamson, India Foils
33	Birla, M.P.	1,702	Birla, Priyamvada	Marwari, Maheshvari	Calcutta	Assam Jute, Universal Cables, Birla Corp.
34	Singhania, V.	1,694	Singhania, Vijaypat	Marwari, Agarwal	Mumbai	Raymond Synthetics, JK Chemicals, JK Helene Curtis
36	Birla, S.K.	1,578	Birla, Sudarshan K.	Marwari, Maheshvari	Calcutta	Birla VXL, Mysore Cements, Sidarth Soya Products
38	Indo Rama	1,397	Lohia, M.L.	Marwari	Delhi	Indo Rama Synthetics, Uniworth International, Woolworth
39	Dalmia, Sanjay	1,393	Dalmia, Sanjay	Marwari, Agarwal, Jain	Delhi	Bharat Explosives, Dalmia Cement, Gujarat Heavy Chemicals
40	Modi	1,357	Modi, Vinay Kumar	Marwari, Agarwal	Delhi	Modi Rubber, Modistone
46	Essar	1,214	Ruia, Sashi	Marwari	Mumbai	Essar Oil, Essar Shipping, Essar Steel, South India Shipping Corp.
50	NEPC	1,161	Khemka, Ravi P.	Marwari, ?	Chennai	NEPC India, NEPC Textiles, South India Cements
II	PARSI	35,463				
1	Tata	31,471	Tata, R.N.	Parsi	Mumbai	TISCO, TELCO
22	Wadia	2,120	Wadia, Nusli	Parsi	Mumbai	Bombay Dyeing, AFCO Industrial, Bombay Burma Trading

No.	Houses	Turn.	Chairman	Community	HQ	Companies
28	Godrej	1,872	Godrej, S.P.	Parsi	Mumbai	Godrej Soaps, G. Hicare, Swadeshi Detergents
III	PUNJABI, KHATRI, ...	18,161				
5	Thapar, L.M.	3,984	Thapar, L.M.	Punjabi, Khatri	Delhi	Karam Chand Thapar & Bros., APR Ltd., Crompton Greaves
8	M & M	3,472	Mahindra, Keshub	Punjabi, Khatri	Mumbai	Mahindra & Mahindra, Mahindra Ugine Steel, Mahindra Engg.
10	Escorts	2,865	Nanda, H.P.	Punjabi	Delhi	Escorts, Escorts Automotives, Escorts JCB, Goetze
20	Usha	2,227	Rai, Vinay	Punjabi, ?	Delhi	Usha India, Gordon Herbert, Information Technologies
27	Siel	1,908	Shriram, Siddharth	Punjabi, Agarwal	Delhi	Shriram Honda Power Equipment, Shriram Pistons, Siel
42	Apollo	1,289	Kanwar, Onkar S.	Punjabi, Sikh	Delhi	Apollo Tyres, Premier Tyres
44	Thapar, M.M.	1,234	Thapar, Man Mohan	Punjabi, Khatri	Delhi	JTC, JTC Electronics
49	Ranbaxy	1,182	Singh, Parvinder	Punjabi, Sikh	Delhi	Ranbaxy Drugs, Ranbaxy Laboratories, Solus Pharmaceuticals
IV	GUJARATI, JAIN, ...	16,915				
3	Ambani	8,468	Ambani, D.H.	Gujarati	Mumbai	Reliance Industries
19	Mafatlal, A.	2,374	Mafatlal, Arvind	Gujarati, Patel	Mumbai	Gujarat Gas, NOCIL, Mafatlal Industries
25	Lalbhai	1,971	Lalbhai, Arvind	Gujarati, Jain	Ahmedabad	Arvind Mills, Atul, Cibatul, Amtrex Appliances

No.	Houses	Turn.	Chairman	Community	HQ	Companies
35	Torrent	1,665	Metha, Uttambhai	Gujarati	Ahmedabad	Ahmedabad Electricity, Surat Electricity, Torrent Cables
45	Doshi, V.	1,226	Doshi, Vinod L.	Gujarati, Jain, Digambara	Mumbai	Premier Auto Electric, Walchandnagar Industries
47	Mukand	1,211	Shah, Viren J.	Gujarati	Mumbai	ISPL Industries, Mukand, Mukand Engineers
V	CHETTIAR NAGARATTAR	6,367				
6	SPIC-MAC	3,896	Chidambaram, M.A.	Chettiar Nagarattar	Chennai	Tamil Nadu Petroproducts, MAC Industries, Manali Petrochemicals
17	Murugappa	2,471	Subbiah, M.V.	Chettiar Nagarattar	Chennai	Carborundum Univ., Cholamandalam Inv., Tube Invests of India
VI	BRAHMIN	6,172				
13	Kirloskar	2,667	Kirloskar, Vijay	Brahmin, Karhada	Bangalore	Kirloskar Bros., K. Copeland, K. Electric, KOEL, K. Pneumatic
31	Lloyds	1,755	Gupta, Raj Narayan	Brahmin	Mumbai	Lloyds Steel Inds., Lloyds Metal & Engineers
32	Amalgamation	1,750	Sivasaliam, A.	Brahmin, Tamil	Chennai	Amco Batteries, Bimetal Bearings, India Pistons, Simpson & Co.
VII	SINDHI	4,523				
12	Jumbo	2,693	Chhabria, M.R.	Sindhi	Dubai	Dunlop India, Falcon Tyres, Maharashtra Distilleries, Shaw Wallace

No.	Houses	Turn.	Chairman	Community	HQ	Companies
29	Hinduja	1,830	Hinduja, S.P.	Sindhi, Shikarpuri	London	Ashok Leyland, Hinduja Finance, Astra-IDL, Gulf Oil India
VIII	OTHERS					
15	UB	2,484	Mallya, Vijay	?	Bangalore	United Breweries, Best & Crompton, Mangalore Chemicals
21	BPL	2,148	Nambiar, T.P.G.	Malayali, Nair	Bangalore	BPL, BPL Engineering, BPL Refrigeration
23	MRF	2,011	Mappilai, K.M.M.	Syrian Christian	Chennai	MRF, Funskool
37	Ruchi	1,435	Shahra, K.C.	?	Indore	Ruchi Soya Industries, R. Strips & Alloys, Madhya Pradesh Glynchem
41	Nagarjuna	1,341	Raju, K.S.	Raju	Hyderabad	Nagarjuna Fertilizers & Chemicals, Nagarjuna Steels
43	Premji	1,287	Premji, Azim H.	Bohra Muslim	Mumbai	Wipro, Wipro Finance
48	Kalyani	1,187	Kalyani, N.A.	?	Pune	Bharat Forge, Automotive Axles, Kalyani Brakes

Source (turnover): *Business Today*, 'India's Business Houses 1947-1997', 22 Aug.–6 Sept. 1997.

Note: Community categories according to increasing order of precision: regional (Gujarati, Malayali or Keralite, Marwari, Punjabi, Tamil), caste (Brahmin), *jati* (Agarwal, Maheshwari, Nagarattar, Raju), religion other than Hindu (Christian, Muslim, Parsi, Sikh, Jain), sect (Bohra, Digambara).

APPENDIX 3

Birla Family Tree

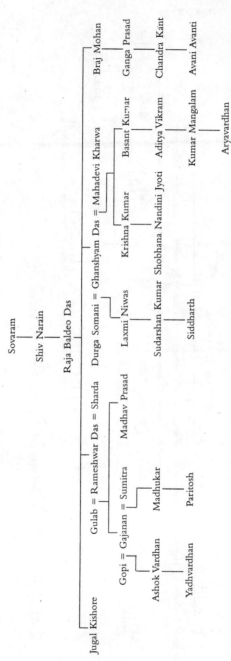

Source: Piramal Gita, *Business Legends*, New Delhi: Penguin Books, 1998.

Godrej Family Tree

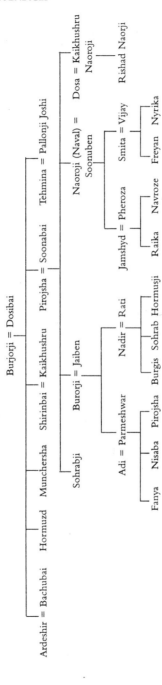

Source: B.J. Karanjia, *Godrej, A Hundred Years (1897-1997)*, New Delhi: Viking, 1997.

Tata Family Tree

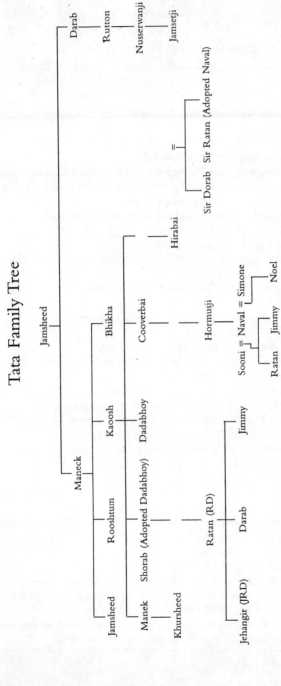

Source: Piramal Gita, *Business Legends*, New Delhi: Penguin Books, 1998.

APPENDIX 4

Chronology of Political Events

Date	Event
1947	Pakistan and India attain Independence. Nehru becomes Prime Minister.
1951	First Five-Year Plan launched. First general elections held.
1952	First general elections concluded.
1955	Avadi session of the Congress party. Resolution adopted which proclaims that the goal of planning is to establish a socialist society.
1956	Second Five-Year Plan launched.
1957	Second general elections held. Nehru re-elected.
1961	Third Five-Year Plan launched.
1962	Third general elections.
1964	Nehru passes away. Lal Bahadur Shastri sworn in as Prime Minister.
1966	Fourth Five-Year Plan launched. Indira Gandhi becomes Prime Minister.
1971	Fifth general elections. Indira Gandhi re-elected.
1974	Fifth Five-Year Plan launched.
1975	Proclamation of Emergency by Indira Gandhi.
1977	End of Emergency. Morarji Desai (Janata Party) becomes Prime Minister.
1978	Formation of Congress-I by Indira Gandhi.
1979	Janata Party breaks up. Resignation of Desai government.
1980	Sixth Five-Year Plan launched. Seventh general elections. BJP born from the 1979 split in the Janata Party.
1984	Eighth general elections. Rajiv Gandhi becomes Prime Minister.
1989	Ninth general elections. V.P. Singh elected Prime Minister.
1990	Eleventh general elections. P.V. Narasimha Rao (Congress-I) becomes Prime Minister. Presents broad outlines of a new, more liberal economic policy before Parliament.
1991	Financial bankruptcy in July and initiation of the Structural Adjustment Plan.
1992	Eighth Five-Year Plan launched.
1997	Ninth Five-Year Plan launched.
1998	Twelfth general elections. Formation of coalition government led by Atal Behari Vajpayee. Continues the economic policies initiated by the Rao government.
1999	Thirteenth general elections. Vajpayee forms another coalition government (24 political formations are represented).

Glossary of Some Political Parties

INDIAN NATIONAL CONGRESS (INC)

Founded in 1885, the Congress party is independent India's oldest political party. It dominated national politics for over five decades, from 1947 to 1997. The Congress-O (O for organization) was born in 1969, from a split in the Congress. Indira Gandhi then created the Congress-R (R for ruling). The Congress-R was backed by a majority of Congressmen; the Congress O was composed of personalities who constituted its regional support base. In 1978, Indira Gandhi founded the Congress(I) (I for Indira). This party remained in power at the Centre almost uninterruptedly until 1996.

BHARATIYA JANA SANGH (BJS)

Formed in 1951, the Jana Sangh defended the interests of nationalist Hindus. Its founders came from the Rashtriya Swayamsevak Sangh (association of Hindu volunteers), founded in 1925. It operates through its regional divisions set up in many of the north Indian states.

JANATA PARTY

An amalgam of left-wing other than non-communist forces, centrist and the right-wing parties, to which were added the former members of the Congress party, that came together during and after the Emergency (1975–7) to form a new Party, the Janata Party. The programmes and policies of the Janata Party were inspired by Charan Singh's agrarian policies that sought to promote agriculture, a self-reliant peasantry and small industries. The Janata Party was strongly in favour of the decentralization of planning. Its finest hour was under Morarji Desai, Prime Minister from 1975 to 1977. However, the Janata Party, a loose coalition of diverse interests underwent too rapid a transformation, which explains its premature demise.

JANATA DAL (JD)

The Janata Dal, one of the political formations that sprang from the Janata Party, made its political debut at the Centre in November 1989, when Vishwanath Pratap Singh became Prime Minister. After its fall from power in December 1990, the party's influence diminished, the principal benefits of which went to the BJP.

BHARATIYA JANATA PARTY (BJP)

Founded in 1980, successor of the Jana Sangh, the BJP claimed to be heir to the values upheld by the Janata Party. Its president, Atal Behari Vajpayee, laid claim to this affiliation by virtue of the attachment of the ex-Jansanghis to the values of the Janata Party. From 1989 to 1992, the BJP turned out to be one of the more dynamic forces in the country. It played the Hindu nationalist card extensively. It constituted its first national government in 1998, but was brought down. It was re-elected in October 1999. Its economic policy is a continuation of the liberalization process started in 1990.

COMMUNIST PARTY OF INDIA (CPI)

Founded in 1925, the Communist Party of India, although classed as a national party in Bengal, has a *de facto* regional character. Particularly influential during the Independence struggle, it is today limited to its bastions of West Bengal, Kerala and Bihar.

COMMUNIST PARTY OF INDIA-MARXIST (CPI-M)

Born in 1964 from a split in the Communist Party of India and known as the CPI-M. It has been in power in West Bengal and the neighbouring state of Tripura for ten years. In 1967, the Communist Party of India Marxist-Leninist, linked with the Naxalbari movement of Maoist leaning, was formed in Bengal.

SWATANTRA PARTY (SWA)

This liberal party made its appearance in the late 1950s. Founded by former Congressmen including C. Rajagopalachari, a leader of the Independence movement, N.G. Ranga, the peasant leader, and K.M. Munshi, together with champions of free enterprise, like R.M. Masani, a former Tata executive who became resolutely anti-Communist. It advocated a curtailing of the role of the state in the economy, a stand that had the approval of business circles and several princes. In 1962, the Swantantra Party won 18 seats in the Lok Sabha with 7.9 per cent votes.

Glossary

agarbati: incense stick that is burnt before religious statues and images

ahimsa: non-violence, doctrine of non-violence

Arjun: hero of the Pandava clan, Krishna's interlocutor in the *Bhagavad Gita*

artha: the second of man's goals, material and political interest

Arthashastra: group of classical texts dealing with *artha*

atman: supreme entity in man, the Self

bania: merchant, merchant caste, in particular Gujarati merchants

Bhagavad Gita: 'The Song of the Lord', philosophico-religious poem in the *Mahabharata*

Bhaktimarga: path to salvation through prayer and love of the divinity

bhoomipuja: ritual conducted at the site of a building prior to starting construction

Brahman: Supreme Being, universal cosmic consciousness, identical to *atman*

Brahmin: priest, sacerdotal order or caste, the first of the *varnas*

burqa: black cape with a black veil hiding the face, worn by Muslim women

chandala: name by which all those considered impure were known in classical texts

clan: lineages of great genealogical depth that claim to have a common first ancestor who may be a mythical figure, and who can be more or less deified

coparcener: term in Anglo-Indian law, undivided property of the Hindu Joint Family

crore: unit of monetary measure equivalent to 10 million or 100 lakh (1 lakh = 1,00,000)

Dussehra: festival in honour of the goddess Durga

Dayabhaga: group of classical juridical texts, school of interpretation of juridical texts, known in Bengal (cf. *Mitakshara*)

dharma: socio-cosmic and moral order, the first of man's goals

dharmadan: charitable donation

Dharmashastra: group of classical texts on *dharma*

darshan: view, 'participative vision' of a temple deity, a saint, etc.

darshana: name given to the six classical systems of the Hindu philosophy

descent group: minor lineage of two to four generations

Digambar: Jain sect whose ascetics go around naked

Diwali (Dipawali): festival towards the end of the year according to the Hindu calendar

Durga: goddess, Shiva's consort who fights against demons

Ganesh(a), Ganapati: god with elephant's head, son of Shiva and Parvati, who removes obstacles

gaddi: cushion of honour, throne, trader's/merchant's seat, extrapolated to mean 'head office'

harijan: 'children of God', name given by Gandhi to 'Untouchables', now termed 'Dalits' or 'Scheduled castes'

hundi: financial instrument, collection box in a temple

hypergamic (alliance): marriage alliance in which the husband belongs to a higher status group than his wife's (particularly in north India)

isogamic (alliance): marriage alliance between relatives from already allied descent groups of equal status (particularly in south India)

Jain, Jainism: religion founded in the sixth–fifth century BC; social group practising this religion (cf. Digambara, Swetambara)

jamaat: community, area depending on a mosque (similar to a parish), religious movement (cf. Tabligh-i Jamaat, Jamaat-i Islami)

Jamaat-i Islami: international Islamic movement founded in India in the late 1950s by Maulana Maududi

jati: endogamous subdivision of a caste, concretely realized social group

Jnanamarg, Dhyanamarga: path to salvation through knowledge, gnosis

Kaliyug: the present era, according to Brahmanical cosmology, the worst era

kama: sensual pleasure, the third of man's goals

Kamasutra: treatise on *kama*

karma: results of actions which decide future reincarnations

karmamarga, karmayoga: salvation through action, social works

karmayogi: one who follows *karmamarga*, or *karmayoga*, or has attained salvation through its practice

karta: head of the Hindu Joint Family, of a firm, or group of family-owned firms

Kaurava: clan fighting the Pandava cousins in the *Mahabharata* and the *Bhagavad Gita*

Krishna: important god, Vishnu's *avatar*, Arjun's interlocutor in the *Bhagavad Gita*

Kshatriya: second *varna*, order, state or class of princes and warriors in classical normative literature

kuldevata, kuldeva(i): clan/family god or goddess

labh: inscription in books of accounts signifying 'good fortune'

Lakshmi: Goddess of wealth and prosperity, Vishnu's consort, who is worshipped particularly during the Diwali festival

lineage: kin descended from a common ancestor

Mahabharata: one of the two major Indian epic poems, of which the *Bhagavad Gita* is a chapter (cf. *Ramayana*)

mandir: temple

marga: path to salvation (cf. *yoga*)

matrilineal: continuity of generations from mother to daughter (particularly in south India)

maya: cosmic illusion, empirical manifestation masking the Brahman

Mitakshara: group of classical juridical texts, school of interpretation of juridical texts (cf. *Dayabhaga*)

moksha: liberation from the human state, realization of the identity of *atman* and Brahman, the highest of man's goals

muthuvelli: administrative head of the *jamaat*

nakshatra: astrological term, constellations and lunar houses

nirvana: Buddhist equivalent of *moksha*

nishkam karma: uninterested action leading to salvation of the *karmamarga* philosophy

panchang: popular name given to the almanacs published each year

Pandava: Arjun's clan which fought the Kaurava cousins' clan in the *Mahabharata* and the *Bhagavad Gita*

patrilineal: continuity of generations from father to son

polygamy: polygyny (one man several wives) or polyandry (one woman and several husbands)

prasad: consecrated food offered to people at the end of a religious ceremony

puja: any worship or ritual

puja room: Anglo-Indian term: room reserved for prayer in the home

punya: acts of merit in the religious sense

purdah: principle of segregation of sexes in social life; interdiction imposed on men outside the immediate family from looking at the women of this family

purushartha: goals of man: *dharma, artha, kama* and *moksha*

Rama: god, hero of the *Ramayana*

Ramayana: one of the two great Indian epic poems whose heroes are Rama and Sita (cf. *Mahabharata*)

samsara: infinite cycles of birth and rebirth governed by the law of *karma*

Samvat: system of dating, calendar starting from 57–56 BC

Sanatana Dharma: eternal *Dharma* (or religion), a concept developed by the neo-Hindu reformist current of the nineteenth century

Sangh Parivar: federation of Hindutva movements, organizations and groupings associated with the Bharatiya Janata Party (BJP)

Saraswati: Goddess of the arts, music and wisdom, linked to the god Brahma

satya: truth, reality, an aspect of the Ultimate Reality

seva: service of the gods; today, it signifies philanthropic works or altruistic action

Shaka: system of dating, calendar starting from 79–78 BC

shakti: female energy, active feminine principle, divinities associated with the gods *shubh*: 'gain, profit' inscribed in the books of accounts, furniture, etc., during the Diwali festival and especially during Lakshmi puja

Shudra: fourth *varna*, i.e. those who are at the service of the first three *varnas*

Sikh: religion or sect born from a blending of Hindu and Muslim principles, founded in 1469 by Nanak and most widespread in the Punjab

swastika: ancient Vedic symbol in the form of a gammadion cross

Swetambara: Jain sect whose followers wear white clothes

swadharma: duty, *dharma* which is specific to a social group (*jati*), or to an individual

swami: title given in sign of respect to masters and to certain religious leaders

Swaminarayan: sect founded in Gujarat towards 1817 by Swami Narayana, many of whose followers are from the merchant communities and from the middle class

Tabligh-i Jamaat: Islamic international movement founded in India in the late 1920s by Maulana Muhammad Ilyas.

Upanishad: group of speculative and philosophical texts, the oldest of which are a continuation of the Vedas

Vaishya: producers, professionals and, above all, merchants, the third *varna*

varna: castes, orders, states or class hierarchies (cf. Brahmin, Vaishya, Kshatriya, Shudra)

vastushastra, vastuvidya: general name given to treatises on art and architecture

Venkateshvaran: Vishnuite deity of the Tirupati temple in Andhra Pradesh

wakf: trust, donations by individuals for the benefit of the community (cf. *jamaat*)

yagna, yagya: sacrifice, sacrificial ritual

Yama: God of Death

yantra: geometrical figure representing the universe, instrument, an aid to meditation

yantra-mandir: here, 'temple of machines'

yantra-yuga: here, 'era of machines', technological era

yoga: philosophical systems and practices teaching the techniques of liberation, path to salvation (cf. *marga*)

yuga: era in the Brahmanical cosmology

Bibliography

Agarwal, Satya P.: 1993. *The Social Role of The Gita, How and Why*, Motilal Banarsidas, New Delhi.

Annussamy, David: 1991. 'La personnalité juridique de l'idole hindoue', *Revue historique de droit français et étranger*, Sirey, Vol. 57, pp. 611–21.

Assayag, Jackie: 1995. *The Making of Democratic Inequality: Caste, Class, Lobbies and Politics in Contemporary India (1880–1995)*, Pondy Papers in Social Sciences No. 18, French Institute of Pondicherry.

Aurobindo, Shri: 1942. *La Bhagavad-Gita* (transl. Camille Rao et Jean Herbert) Preface by Jean Herbert, Albin Michel, Paris, rpt. 1970.

Bana, Sarosh: 1999. 'Steady it Grows', 23 Aug.–5 Sept., p. 101.

Bayly, Susan: 1999. *Caste, Society and Politics in India From The Eighteenth Century to The Modern Age*, The New Cambridge History of India, Cambridge University Press, Cambridge.

Birla, G.D.: 1944. *The Plan Explained*, Bombay.

Boltanski, Luc and Thévenot, Laurent: 1991. *De la justification. Les économies de la grandeur*, nrf essais, Gallimard, Paris.

Business India: 1984. 'Temple Trusts: The Case of Tirupati', 10–23 Sept., pp. 86–95.

————: 1995. *Business India, Super 100*, 23 Oct.

————: 1997. 'Temples are Business Assets', 27 Jan.–9 Feb., p. 157.

Business Today: 1998. 'India's Business Families: Can They Survive?', Special Double Issue, 7 Jan.–6 Feb.

————: 1997. 'India's Business Houses 1947–1997', 22 Aug.–6 Sept.

Business World: 1988. 'The Maharishi and His Millions', 7–21 Oct., pp. 114–15.

Cadène, Philippe and Holmström, Mark (ed.): 1998. *Decentralized Production in India*, Sage, New Delhi.

Chakrabarti, Vibhuti: 1999. *Indian Architectural Theory. Contemporary Uses of Vastu Vidya*, Oxford University Press, Mumbai.

Chakraborty, S.K.: 1995. *Ethics in Management. Vedantic Perspectives*, Oxford University Press, New Delhi (paperback 1996).

————: 1987. *Managerial Effectiveness and Quality of Work-life. Indian Insights*, Tata–McGraw-Hill, New Delhi.

Chentsal Rao, P.: 1986. *Lakshmipat Singhania, His Concepts and Creations*, Vikas, New Delhi.

Desai, Ashok V.: 1992. 'The Origins of Parsi Enterprise', in Rajat Kanta Ray (ed.), *Entrepreneurship and Industry in India 1800–1947*, Oxford University Press, New Delhi, pp. 99–108.

Desai, Rajiv: 1999. *Indian Business Culture*, Viva Books, New Delhi.

Dhanuka, Amishi (ed.): 1996. *A Chronicle of Marwari History and Achievements*, Marwar, Arpan Publishing, Mumbai, Vol. 1.

Diwan, Paras and Peeyushi Diwan: 1995. *Hindu Law*, Wadhwa & Company, Allahabad.

Doniger, Wendy with Brian K. Smith (trs.): 1991. *The Laws of Manu*, Penguin Books, New Delhi.

Dorin, Bruno: 1994. *L'économie oléifère de l'Union Indienne. Evaluation d'une stratégie d'autonomie'*, Ph.D. thesis, Université Montpellier I.

Dorin, Bruno, Flamant, Nicolas, Lachaier, Pierre and Vaugier-Chatterjee, Anne: 2000. *Le Patronat en Inde. Contours sociologiques des acteurs et des pratiques*, Centre de Sciences Humaines, New Delhi.

Dumont, Louis: 1966. *Homo hierarchicus*, Gallimard, Paris.

Dupuis, Jacques: 1969. *Madras et le Nord Coromandel*, Librairie d'Amérique et d'Orient, Adrien Maisonneuve, Paris.

Dutta, Sudipt: 1997. *Family Business in India*, Response Books, Sage, New Delhi.

Engineer, A.A.: 1989. *The Muslim Communities of Gujarat. An Explanatory Study of Bohras, Khojas and Memons*, Ajanta, New Delhi.

Erdman, Howard L.: 1967. *The Swatantra Party and Indian Conservatism*, Cambridge University Press, Cambridge.

Fortune India: 1996. 'Licence to Kill', 15 Sept.

Frankel, Francine: 1978. *India's Political Economy (1947–1977)*, Princeton University Press, Princeton.

Gandhi, M.K.: 1982. *Autobiographie ou mes expériences de vérité*, 3rd edn., PUF, Paris.

Giddens, Anthony: 1992. *Les conséquences de la modernité*, L'Harmattan, Paris.

Grewal, J.S.: 1984. 'Business Communities of Punjab', in D. Tripathi (ed.), *Business Communities of India. A Historical Perspective*, Manohar, New Delhi, pp. 186–209.

Guha, Amendu: 1984. 'More about the Parsee Sheths, 1650-1918', in D. Tripathi (ed.), *Business Communities of India. A Historical Perspective*, Manohar, New Delhi, pp. 109–50.

Gurcharan Das: 1996. 'Divided we may fall, But united we are unassailable', in Amishi Dhanuka (ed.), *A Chronicle of Marwari History and Achievements*, Marwar, Arpan Publishing, Mumbai, Vol. 1, pp. 72–81.

———: 1999. 'The Problem', in *Seminar, Family Business*, No. 482, Oct., pp. 12–21.

Hanson, A.H.: 1966. *The Process of Planning*, Oxford University Press, London.

Harris, Frank: 1958. *Jamsetji, Nusserwanji Tata. A Chronicle of His Life*, Blackie and Sons, Mumbai.

Haynes, Douglas E.: 1987. 'From Tribute to Philanthropy: The Politics of Gift Giving in a Western Indian City', *The Journal of Asian Studies*, May, pp. 339–60.

Humbert, Philippe: 1990. *Inde. Les Années Rajiv Gandhi (1984–1989)*, L'Harmattan, Paris.

Jaffrelot, Christophe: 1998. *La Démocratie en Inde*, Fayard, Paris.

Jaju, Ram Niwas: 1985. *G.D. Birla. A Biography*, Vikas, New Delhi.

Jalan, Bimal: 1992. *The Indian Economy. Problems and Prospects*, Viking, New Delhi.

Jhabvala Noshirvan, H.: 1996. *Principles of Hindu Law*, 18th rev. edn., C. Jamnadas & Co., Bombay.

Kamath, M.V.: 1995. *Gandhi's Coolie. Life and Times of Ramakrishna Bajaj*, Allied, New Delhi.

Karanjia, B.J.: 1997. *Godrej, A Hundred Years (1897–1997)*, Vol. 1, 2, Viking, New Delhi.

Karve, Iravati: 1993. 'The Kinship Map of India', in Patricia Uberoi (ed.), *Family, Kinship and Marriage in India*, Oxford University Press, New Delhi, pp. 50–73.

Kirloskar, S.L.: 1982. *Cactus and Roses. An Autobiography by Kirloskar S.L.*, xii, C.G. Phadke, Pune.

————: 1983. *Selected Speeches and Writings*, C.G. Phadke, Pune.

Kochanek, Stanley: 1974. *Business and Politics in India*, University of California Press, Berkeley.

Kulke, Eckehard: 1978. *The Parsees in India. A Minority as Agent of Social Change*, Vikas, New Delhi (Weltforum Verlag GmbH. Munich 1974).

Lachaier, Pierre: 1993. 'Vers un management hindou? Présentation et analyse du livre de S.K. Chakraborty "Managerial Effectiveness and Quality of Worklife, Indian Insights"', *Gérer et Comprendre*, Annales des Mines, Dec., No. 33, pp. 56–63.

————: 1999. *Firmes et entreprises en Inde. La firme lignagère dans ses réseaux*, EFEO–IFP–Karthala, Paris.

Lala, R.M.: 1995. *Beyond the Last Blue Mountain. A Biography of J.R.D. Tata (1904–1993)*, Viking Books, New Delhi.

Madan, T.N.: 1993. 'The Hindu Family and Development', in Patricia Uberoi (ed.), *Family, Kinship and Marriage in India*, Oxford University Press, New Delhi, pp. 416–34.

Markovits, Claude: 1985. *Indian Business and Nationalist Politics, 1931–39*, Cambridge University Press, Cambridge.

————: 1981. 'Indian Business and the Congress Provincial Governments, 1937–39', *Modern Asian Studies*, XV.

Mahratta Chamber of Commerce and Industries: 1984. *Who's Who in Pune Industry*, Pune.

Meshrovb, Jacob Sheth: 1983. *Armenians in India, From the Earliest Times to the Present Day. A Work of Original Research*, Oxford & IBH, New Delhi, rpt.

Milbert, Isabelle: 1981. *L'Inde. Evolution Politique, Economique et Sociale*, Notes et études documentaires, Nos. 4639–40, la Documentation Française, Paris.

Mines, Matison: 1978. 'Social Stratification among Muslims in Tamil Nadu', in Imtiaz Ahmad (ed.), *Castes and Social Stratifications among Muslims in India*, Manohar, New Delhi.

Nayar, Baldev Raj: 1989. *India's Mixed Economy*, New Delhi.

Nishimura, Yuko: 1998. *Gender, Kinship and Property Rights*, Oxford University Press, New Delhi.

Papanek, Hanna: 1973. 'Pakistan's New Industrialists and Businessmen: Focus on the Memmons', in Milton Singer (ed.), *Entrepreneurship and Modernization of Occupational Cultures in South Asia*, Comparative Studies on Southern Asia, Monograph No. 12, Duke University, Durham.

Piramal, Gita: 1996. 'In The Pursuit of Laxmi', in Amishi Dhanuka (ed.), *A Chronicle of Marwari History and Achievements*, Marwar, Arpan Publishing, Mumbai, Vol. 1, pp. 91–7.

————: 1996. *Business Maharajas*, Viking, New Delhi.

————: 1999. *Business Legends*, Penguin Books India, New Delhi.

————: 2000. 'The Rise and Fall of Clans', *Business World*, 3 Jan., pp. 35–6.

Pocock, D.F.: 1993. 'The Hypergamy of the Patidars', in Patricia Uberoi (ed.), *Family, Kinship and Marriage in India*, Oxford University Press, New Delhi, pp. 330–40.

Ray, Rajat Kanta (ed.): 1992. *Entrepreneurship and Industry in India 1800–1947*, Oxford University Press, New Delhi.

Rudner, David West: 1995. *Caste and Capitalism in Colonial India. The Nattukottai Chettiars*, Munshiram Manoharlal, New Delhi.

Rudolph, Lloyd I. and Susanne Rudolph: 1987. *In Pursuit of Lakshmi. The Political Economy of the Indian State*, Orient Longman, New Delhi.

Sainsaulieu, Renaud (ed.): 1990. *L'entreprise, une affaire de société*, Presses de la Fondation Nationale des Sciences Politiques, Paris.

Seminar: 1999. 'Family Business', No. 482, Oct.

Shamasastry, R.: 1967. *Kautilya's Arthashastra*, rpt., Mysore Printing and Pub. House, Mysore.

Shrinivas, M.N. et al.: 1966. 'A Sociological Study of Okhla Industrial Estate', in *Small Industries and Social Change*, New Delhi, UNESCO Research Center.

Singer, M.: 1968. 'The Indian Joint Family in Modern Industry', in B.S. Cohn and M. Singer (ed.), *Structure and Change in Indian Society*, Chicago University Press, Chicago, pp. 423–52.

————: 1972. *When a Great Tradition Modernizes. An Anthropological Approach to Indian Civilization,* Vikas, New Delhi.

Singh, K.S. (ed.): 1998. *India's Communities,* People of India Series, Anthropological Survey of India, Vol. IV A–G, Vol. V H–M, Vol. VI N–Z, Oxford University Press, New Delhi.

Singh, N.K.: 1986. '800 kg Ghee Burnt to "Purify" Bhopal!', *Indian Express,* Bombay, 14 Jan.

Singhania, Hari Shankar: 1995. *Economic Issues Global & National. A Business Perspective,* Vikas, New Delhi.

Sinha, Dharni P.: 1991. *Business Scenarios for the 90s. Strategic Perspectives,* Vikas, New Delhi.

Sridharan, E.: 1999. 'Toward State Funding of Elections in India? A Comparative Perspective on Possible Options', *Policy Reform,* Vol. 3, Oct., pp. 229–54.

Subramaniam, V.: 1971. *The Managerial Class of India,* All India Management Association, New Delhi.

Tata, J.R.D.: 1971. 'The Future of the Private Sector', *Journal of The Indian Merchant's Chamber.*

Thingalaya, N.K.: 1999. *The Banking Saga. History of South Kanara Banks,* Corporation Bank Economic Development Foundation, Mangalore.

Tirmizi, S.A.I.: 1984. 'Muslim Merchants of Medieval Gujarat', in D. Tripathi (ed.), *Business Communities of India. A Historical Perspective,* Manohar, New Delhi.

Todd, James Col.: 1914. *Annals and Antiquities of Rajasthan.*

Trautmann, Th. R.: 1993. 'The Study of Dravidian Kinship', in Patricia Uberoi (ed.), *Family, Kinship and Marriage in India,* Oxford University Press, New Delhi, pp. 74–90.

Tripathi, D. and M.J. Metha: 1984. 'Class Character of the Gujarati Business Community', in D. Tripathi (ed.), *Business Communities of India. A Historical Perspective,* Manohar, New Delhi, pp. 151–70.

Tripathi, Dwijendra (ed.): 1981. *The Dynamics of a Tradition. Kasturbhai Lalbhai and His Entrepreneurship,* Manohar, New Delhi.

————: 1984. *Business Communities of India. A Historical Perspective,* Manohar, New Delhi.

————: 1990. *Business Houses in Western India. A Study in Entrepreneurial Response, 1850–1956,* Manohar, New Delhi.

————: 1991. *Business and Politics in India. A Historical Perspective,* Manohar, New Delhi.

————: 1999. 'Change and Continuity', in *Seminar,* 'Family Business', No. 482, Oct., pp. 29–32.

Trivedi, M.L.: 1980. *Government and Business,* Multi-tech Publishing Co., Bombay.

Uberoi, Patricia (ed.): 1993. *Family, Kinship and Marriage in India,* Oxford University Press, New Delhi.

Venkatasubbaiah, H.: 1977. *Enterprise and Economic Change: 50 Years of FICCI*, Vikas, New Delhi.

Venou, Fabienne: 1999. 'Le mariage à l'épreuve du travail en usine: ouvrières de l'industrie de la chaussure en Inde du Sud', *Journal des anthropologues*, No. 77–8, pp. 123–40.

Zins, Max-Jean: 1992. *Histoire politique de l'Inde indépendante*, PUF, Paris.

Index